413/298-3239

D0057057

Daddy's Boy

Daddy's Boy

A SON'S SHOCKING ACCOUNT
OF LIFE WITH A FAMOUS FATHER

CHRIS ELLIOTT
WITH REBUTTALS BY
BOB ELLIOTT

**Delacorte
Press**

Published by
Delacorte Press
Bantam Doubleday Dell Publishing Group, Inc.
666 Fifth Avenue
New York, New York 10103

"The Haddock Thinks He's Better Than the Cod," on page 136, is from a series of verses entitled *Fish Have Their Problems Too* by William C. Roux, © 1964. Reprinted by permission, Yankee Magazine, Dublin, N.H.

"Tea for the Tillerman," written by Cat Stevens, © 1970. Published by Cat Music Ltd./Westbury Music Consultants Inc. Reprinted by permission.

"The Morning After," written by Al Kasha and Joel Hirshhorn, © 1972 WB Music Corp. & Warner-Tamerlane Publishing Corp. All rights reserved. Used by permission.

"Aqualung," written by Ian Anderson, © 1970. Lyrics reprinted by permission of Chrysalis Music Group and Ian Anderson Music.

Copyright © 1989 by Chris Elliott and Bob Elliott

All rights reserved. No part of this book may be reproduced or transmitted in any form or by any means, electronic or mechanical, including photocopying, recording, or by any information storage and retrieval system, without the written permission of the Publisher, except where permitted by law.

The trademark Delacorte Press ® is registered in the U.S. Patent and Trademark Office.

Library of Congress Cataloging in Publication Data

Elliott, Chris, 1960—
  Daddy's boy.
    1. Elliott, Bob— Humor. 2. Fathers and sons—Humor.
I. Elliott, Bob. II. Title.
PN6162.E47 1989 818′ .5402 89-1100
ISBN 0-385-29730-0

Manufactured in the United States of America
Published simultaneously in Canada
June 1989
10 9 8 7 6 5 4 3 2 1

BG

A SON'S SHOCKING ACCOUNT
OF LIFE WITH A FAMOUS FATHER

CHRIS ELLIOTT
WITH REBUTTALS BY
BOB ELLIOTT

**Delacorte
Press**

Published by
Delacorte Press
Bantam Doubleday Dell Publishing Group, Inc.
666 Fifth Avenue
New York, New York 10103

"The Haddock Thinks He's Better Than the Cod," on page 136, is from a series of verses entitled *Fish Have Their Problems Too* by William C. Roux, © 1964. Reprinted by permission, Yankee Magazine, Dublin, N.H.

"Tea for the Tillerman," written by Cat Stevens, © 1970. Published by Cat Music Ltd./Westbury Music Consultants Inc. Reprinted by permission.

"The Morning After," written by Al Kasha and Joel Hirshhorn, © 1972 WB Music Corp. & Warner-Tamerlane Publishing Corp. All rights reserved. Used by permission.

"Aqualung," written by Ian Anderson, © 1970. Lyrics reprinted by permission of Chrysalis Music Group and Ian Anderson Music.

Copyright © 1989 by Chris Elliott and Bob Elliott

All rights reserved. No part of this book may be reproduced or transmitted in any form or by any means, electronic or mechanical, including photocopying, recording, or by any information storage and retrieval system, without the written permission of the Publisher, except where permitted by law.

The trademark Delacorte Press ® is registered in the U.S. Patent and Trademark Office.

Library of Congress Cataloging in Publication Data

Elliott, Chris, 1960—
   Daddy's boy.
   1. Elliott, Bob— Humor. 2. Fathers and sons—Humor.
I. Elliott, Bob. II. Title.
PN6162.E47 1989 818' .5402 89-1100
ISBN 0-385-29730-0

Manufactured in the United States of America
Published simultaneously in Canada
June 1989
10 9 8 7 6 5 4 3 2 1

BG

Acknowledgments

Editor: Bob Miller

Art Director: Victor Weaver

Photo Illustrations by Bill Shortridge

Graphics Coordinator: Edd Hall

Photos by Peter Cunningham, Barbara Gaines, Lee K. Elliott, and Lynn Goldsmith

Stock photos supplied by Wide World Photos, Inc.

Special thanks to Laurie Lennard

and

Barbara Sheehan, Ken Cichy, Elliot Groffman, Donick Cary, Adam Resnick, Dave Rygalski, Kevin Kay, Maria Pope, Jay Johnson, Peter Montagna, Michael DiCesare, David Letterman, Lee K. Elliott, and Paula Niedert Elliott.

To Daddy, I write this book to purge
us both of the dark ghosts of our past.
The truth will set us free!

Your loving son,
Chris

To Chris, for galvanizing the completion
of this exercise in time for me to
participate in National Family Bread
Baking Month.

Your loving father,
Bob

Foreword
David Letterman

WHEN I FIRST MET CHRIS ELLIOTT, he was a broken man, and I guess that's what I liked about him. I didn't have to waste a lot of my time and energy tearing him down and shredding his self-esteem so he would do my bidding without regard for matters of his own pride or welfare.

I must say, for all his outward manifestations of dull, blunt, coarse stupidity, Chris actually possessed, as our tests revealed, a very high below-average intelligence. And it was in no time at all that you could send him out for gum (never lunch) with some measure of confidence that you'd see him again that day. He also seemed to have a certain native curiosity about life.

"Mr. Letterman?"

"Yes, Chris?"

"What's the difference between soup and gravy?"

So you see, it's not like he was just a box of parts.

I, of course, being in show business, had always heard of the Great Bob Elliott, but for some reason it never occurred to me that Chris was his son. For one thing, despite my earlier tact, he really was just a dolphin in shoes. And for another, I thought all the Elliott punks, or whatever they were called, were named Bob, Jr. I remember when I learned that Chris was the son of the Great Bob Elliott, I assumed it was simply an ill-considered late-life adoption. I still think that was the case, perhaps even linked to some kind of wager gone sour.

Anyway, Chris worked for me for the better part of seven years before we had to let him go. You know, in retrospect it wasn't really his stealing that was the problem. To a guy like me, petty cash is pretty much just that. And, of course, if he wanted the stereo, the pony, and a few big-screen TVs badly enough to yank them out of my office or home, well then, so what. No, I think truly the reason we had to let Chris go—and my security people told me all the profiles supported that decision—were the flowers. For his part, Chris said it was just a big-brother kind of thing, and maybe so. But I feel pretty certain that if I had a big brother, I would not, on a regular basis, be sending him dozens and dozens of long-stemmed red roses just because I was "thinking of you," or whatever the hell the cards said. So we parted company. (As always, I left the actual firing to my manager, Colonel Parker.)

I never really heard from Elliott again. Oh, occasionally there would be the anonymous calls threatening to kill this one or that one if I didn't do so-and-so. I guess we all quietly knew it was Chris, but again, why make trouble?

And now he's written this book with his so-called father, the Great Bob Elliott. I couldn't be more certain that it won't do well. My attorneys skimmed the pages for any mention of me, and I'm told that there is nothing actionable, so in return for some "expense money" I agreed to waste a couple of pages for the kid.

In Chris's case I guess what we're all really concerned about is preventing another Jodie Foster deal. Anyway, he hasn't hurt anyone yet, so as we say in show business, enjoy!

Prologue

"**M**Y NAME IS CHRIS ELLIOTT AND I'M A . . . I'm a . . . a . . ."

The words would not come out. My tongue froze solid in my mouth. Somewhere deep in the back of my brain, the little shop, which for lo these many years had manufactured every syllable and lovingly assembled every sentence by hand, now slammed shut its doors and put out a CLOSED FOR THE HOLIDAYS! sign. If I wanted any more sentences, I would have to break into the little shop and steal the words like a common criminal, and that was just not my style. Instead, I decided to wait it out. I stood there forever, abandoned by my tongue, alone in the limbo of my embarrassment . . . sweating and shaking, sweating and shaking.

"It's all right, Mr. Elliott. We're all friends here." The woman's voice pierced the awkward silence and sounded reassuring. "You can say it. I know you can!" She sat on a folding chair at the head of the room, exuding an air of predominance and authority that both challenged and engaged me. She filled me with a plucky confidence, which automatically reopened the doors to the little syllable shop in my brain, and I was certain I could now finish my sentence: "Yes, my name is Chris Elliott and I am a—"

I stopped. I have to admit that being center stage, being in the spotlight, being this thick-ribbed woman's total investment for the moment was quite alluring, and I chose to milk the opportunity for everything it was worth. "No, I just can't say it. I just can't!" I lamented, and managed to work up some salty tears.

"It's all right, Mr. Elliott, just take your time," she offered. "Everyone in this room knows how difficult this is for you, but we've all had to get past this stage. You have to understand that this is the first step in your recovery."

"I know, I know," I said, grieving, and buried my face in my palms.

There was no telling how long everyone in the room would put up with me. After all, I had attended many of these meetings and was still unable to admit my problem. I peered out through my fingers and scanned the cinder-block basement, filled with the twelve brave souls whose faces were now quite familiar to me but whose names I still hadn't bothered to learn. These were twelve brave souls indeed, for they had all faced their demons and were trying their damnedest to extravasate the poison from their systems. Now it was my turn.

"I just need a second," I whimpered, basking in the room's undivided attention. I was a little surprised how easily the tears flowed, and I thought perhaps some of Daddy's theatrical talents had rubbed off on me, after all.

14

Prologue

"You have to forgive me. I'm not used to this sort of thing," I hiccuped through my tears.

"Of course you're not," said the woman at the front of the room. "None of us were, but we're all here with you, Mr. Elliott . . . and we can help you, if you will start to help yourself."

I dropped my arms to my sides and immediately my hand was met with the warm clasp of a hand belonging to an extravagantly beautiful brunette seated to my right. She looked up at me, her eyes red-rimmed from tears, and she spoke softly and sympathetically. "It's all right, I'll help you, Chris." I could actually see my reflection in her bloodshot, big, brown windows, and I pouted ever so cutely and mouthed "Thank you."

Suddenly I felt something really hot and clammy, and a guy who looked a lot like magician Doug Henning was squeezing my other hand. "I just want to help you, too, Chris!" he shouted, and he jumped to his feet and threw his sleeveless arms around my body, trapping me in a tight, greasy bear hug. "There, doesn't that feel better?" he asked, loosening his hold.

"Yeah, sure, it feels great, buddy. Why don't you just sit back down."

"Damn it, Mr. Elliott, just say it!" the woman's command bellowed forth from the front of the room. "You couldn't be in a safer environment. Get over this hump and get on with your life. You've been coming to these meetings for months now. You've listened to everyone else, but you refuse to say a word. Let tonight be a new beginning! Now, either you crap or you get off the damn pot!"

15

It was "tough love," and it was exactly what I needed. The electromagnetism in her voice shocked me out of my self-indulgent crying act and I remembered that I had come to the meetings for a real reason. I *did* have a problem. I *did* need help. I *did* need love and support. "Oh, God, give me the strength to say these simple words!"

"My name is Chris Elliott, and I use minoxidil!"

The room filled with laughter. I had broken the tension, which was my aim, but when my eyes met with the stern glare of the woman at the front of the room, I knew I would not be allowed to cop out with a cheap laugh.

"All right, I'm ready." I straightened up, inhaled a deep chestful of oxygen, and began: "My name is Chris Elliott, and I am a . . ."

In the second between "I am a . . ." and the rest of that sentence, my mind raced through catalogs of memories, baskets of dreams, voices and colors and images, all from my past. My emotions tugged on heartstrings that had been left untuned and slack for so many years, and a mixed-up kaleidoscope of days gone by flooded my soul. Why was I in that room? What had brought me to that point?

No matter how many times I went over it in my mind—forget everything else—it always came down to one ultimate cause: Daddy. Daddy was my problem. For weeks prior to all this, I had been plagued with horrible nightmares. I would bolt upright in bed, drenched in sweat and screaming at the top of my lungs: "Bob Elliott! Bob Elliott! Bob Elliott!" or "After-shave! After-shave! After-shave!" or "Blue blazers! Blue blazers! Blue blazers!" and there in the eternity of that short second between "My name is Chris Elliott and I am a . . ." and the rest of that sentence, I began to put things in order; it was Daddy all along. It was his presence in the deepest regions of my psyche that still tormented my soul. It was his legacy that I was still imprisoned by, and it was the upbringing (under his rule) that had scarred me permanently. I thought how ironic it was that the man's public image was so contrary to the real Bob Elliott, and I suppose even then, at that moment, I felt the truth had to be told.

I now think that perhaps it was not Daddy's fault entirely. "Fame" played a major role in our troubles and cast the deciding vote in our destinies. Fame fueled our egos, Daddy's and mine, and in the end it was fame that was our most intoxicating addition. Fame, like fire to paper, ruined us.

There used to be a television show called *Fame*, and I remember once sitting with Daddy and watching almost an entire episode and asking him if the program's theme of fresh-faced, bright-eyed young-sters struggling for fame and fortune in the big city struck a nerve with him, as it had with me. "Oh, I don't know about that," he growled. "But I will tell you this much. The kid who played the tuba was the best of the bunch!" That was one of the few heart-to-heart talks Daddy and I ever shared, and it was so indicative of the philosophy that pervaded our household. Fame was a sacred treasure. It was to be worshiped and held dear. You just didn't screw with fame!

Fame, for me, was fleeting. Like Frank Sinatra, Jr., Hank Williams, Jr., Gary Crosby, and all of Martin

Sheen's kids, I've been forced to spend a life working to live up to expectations that I was burdened with unnecessarily. You can't grow up the son of the Great Bob Elliott without feeling some aftershocks, and for weeks prior to the turning point in that cinderblock basement, the aftershocks had been registering 8.9 on the Richter scale of my nerves. I knew things were coming to a head. I knew I had to extravasate the poisons from *my* system. Daddy's hold on my soul would only begin to give a little if I could finish that damn sentence: "My name is Chris Elliott and I am . . . a son of a celebrity!"

There, I said it. I said it out loud. I shouted it, in fact, and it felt great! It was a catharsis of sorts, the first step in the lavation of my spirit. It was like lathering up my emotions with Irish Spring deodorant soap and then washing away the years of filth in a cool shower. It was my declaration of war on the overpowering army of my past, and it felt so good, I had to say it again.

"My name is Chris Elliott and I am a son of a celebrity! The son of a damn celebrity! That's what I am!"

Oh, God, I felt clean. It was like the re-genesis of soil left scraped and barren by a dust-bowl wind. I could feel the buds of life sprouting anew within my tired, eroded veins, and I felt I had experienced firsthand the sensation of biting into a York Peppermint Patty without ever having done so. It was, for me, the light at the end of the tunnel, the dark tunnel of my life, and I was so excited, I began to hyperventilate.

I think in retrospect I should have taken greater notice of the dead silence that hung all around me at that particular moment in the basement room, but I was too caught up in my own consummation. It was a very proud moment for me. I do remember a couple of people clapping politely, but they stopped immediately, as no one else joined in.

"Thank you, thank you very much" I said, acknowledging the weak applause and trying to catch my breath. "Gosh, I feel so much better already. I've been living with this thing bottled up inside of me for so long now. It just feels great to get it out in the open. It's like a giant weight has been lifted from my shoulders, and I have everyone in this room to thank!"

The sympathetic expression on the face of the beautiful brunette with the big brown eyes had now been replaced by a perplexed frown. The guy who looked like Doug Henning was agitated, pounding his knees with his fists. From behind me I heard someone mutter, "Jerk!" and the voice of the woman at the front of the room was icy and unemotional.

"Mr. Elliott," she began, "are you aware that this is a meeting of Alcoholics Anonymous?"

"Well, I was aware that a lot of people in this room have a serious drinking problem, if that's what you mean," I said.

"Do *you* have a serious drinking problem, Mr. Elliott?"

"Of course not!"

"Then why the hell are you wasting our time?"

"Wasting your time?" I snapped incredulously. "Ma'am, I don't think my problem is a waste of time! You know what I think a 'waste of time' is? I think some of the bellyaching I've listened to in this room for the last few months could be considered a *waste of time!*"

"Mr. Elliott, that is enough." She sounded like a teacher fed up with her student's childish behavior.

"Look, I'm sorry I'm not an alcoholic. So sue me! I just happen to be that rare breed of person who can control himself. I can have one or two Rob Roys without the urge to drink myself into total oblivion, like some people I know!"

I should have stopped right there, but I didn't. "I mean, I really feel for you folks, but I gotta tell ya, I just don't relate. All I can say is, just don't drink so much! If you're at a bar or a party, just *control* yourselves, that's all! Now, I'm sorry, but I think I have a *real* problem. I'm sure you all know who Bob Elliott is?"

Silence.

". . . well, he's my father. Are you starting to get the picture? I just had nowhere else to turn."

I began to plead my case, and as I did so, real tears began to stream from my piercing blue eyes. I was in pain, and I was letting it all out.

"You have no idea what it's like to be the son of someone famous . . . to live in the shadow of a legend. It's never just been Chris Elliott; it's always been Chris Elliott, son of the fabulous Bob Elliott. That alone is enough reason for me to be here."

I had never been bodily removed from anywhere before, and when I hit the cold, hard concrete outside, I felt humiliated and alone.

". . . and don't come back," shouted the Doug Henning guy, and then it began to rain.

I'm still not sure whether it was a quest for adventure or just plain stupidity that led me to those AA meetings about a year ago. Somehow I knew I didn't belong.

That night I wandered the streets of Manhattan Island in the pouring rain, and all night long I thought about Daddy, and about my horrifying past. I meandered up to the George Washington Bridge and gazed across the river at the magnificent Palisades, where once the famous MANHATTAN sign had been a magnet for so many "would-be" celebrities back in New York's glory years. I strolled down Broadway, reading all the superstars' names embedded in the concrete sidewalk below my feet: John Wayne, Bette Davis, Bob Elliott (but no Chris Elliott). I walked over to Madison Avenue, where the old Brown Derby Restaurant used to be and shivered in the cold, reminiscing about the night Daddy took me there for a special dinner. I remember our sky-blue Pacer pulling up and the chauffeur opening the door, and then Daddy being mobbed by hundreds of screaming teenage girls. They literally ripped off every article of clothing he had on. But, true to his "public image" at the time, the "doting father" would not postpone dinner with his favorite son. Instead he chose to dine stark naked, ignoring the boisterous complaints of many of the other restaurant patrons. That was Daddy. The Daddy of my past.

I knew I had to do something. I knew I had to get it out of me. But how? How could I make people listen to me? How could I tell the story that so desperately needed telling, and maybe make a few bucks in the process, and then it hit me like a ton of bricks. Write a book! Get it out for Father's Day! Go on all the talk shows! The possibilities and rewards for such effort seemed endless. But wait a second, was I nuts? Did I really have enough complaints about growing up to fill a book? I convinced myself that that didn't matter. The only important thing was that I get my face on the cover.

And so my friends, I retreated to my lovely, two-story, reproduction Cape in Spanish Harlem and began to write this book, *Daddy's Boy: A Son's Shocking Account of Life with a Famous Father.* I warn you that it is tough, frank, and often hard-hitting reading, but it is the total expurgation of my soul. I have been born again! Now, when I walk aimlessly through the streets of Manhattan, I can shout out loud without hesitation: "My name is Chris Elliott and I am a fabulous guy!"

A Note
to My Readers

I APOLOGIZE UP FRONT FOR THE IN-trusion of my father's rebuttals, but it seems that Daddy could sue the pants off me for writing this book, and so my law-yers said he had to get every other chapter to refute my charges. It is an unfortunate situation—one that I am not in the least bit happy about—but alas, it is the way it has to be. All I can say, Dear Reader, is to please remember the source when skimming through his rebuttals. My Dad is like a demon, and he will mix lies with the truth in order to confuse you. I pray you be advised. I also think he's been eating a lot of canned food lately, and he may have gone nuts from lead poisoning.

With that aside, I bid you welcome! Welcome to the world of power, greed, lust, fame, and fortune . . . of gluttony and gastronomy, of concupiscence and morosis, pelf and amentia and pauperism and lycanthropy. . . . Welcome my dear friends, to the world of Daddy's Boy!

23

Rebuttal to Prologue

IT'S EARLY AFTERNOON ON THE sprawling deck commanding the sunny side of my vacation home on the upper shores of Casco Bay.

Heron gulls, gray and grizzled, float with no seeming purpose against a cerulean sky. Hummingbirds dart among blossoms that overgrow the steps leading to the beach. The sun bathes a glistening sea, still winter-cold and bubbling, the air rich with the promising first fresh smells of summer in Maine.

Even now, at a flea market opened a week too early by some overeager entrepreneur, a lone customer is pondering the purchase of an imitation china ashtray, inscribed "We don't swim in your toilet. Please don't pee in our pool."

Lobstermen carry on their daily pursuit of the quarry lurking in and around the nearby islands; beyond them, the wide expanse of horizon is broken at dead center by the lonely lighthouse tower of Halfway Rock, ten miles out.

Rebuttal to Prologue

It is the ideal time—the ideal place—to begin a change-of-pace summer. A vacation combined with work.

I've had a pet project in mind for years now, but for one reason or another, I have been forced to postpone it again and again. This summer, though, I think I can finally give my full attention to it and really get the endeavor off the ground or forget it forever.

Perhaps, by season's end, I will have laid the groundwork for what may turn out to be my greatest promotion idea yet. The first annual Maine Finnan Haddie Festival.

A hundred miles southwest at Kittery, the vehicles of the people "from away" are beginning to form long lines at the tollbooths. Impatiently, drivers grab at the ticket dispenser and speed off onto the turnpike, Interstate 95.

In Maine, the lead story on every radio and television newscast Memorial Day weekend is: "Authorities estimate thirty-five hundred cars an hour are pouring into the state through the Kittery tollbooths."

It's the same on Fourth of July weekend and over Labor Day. At the end of the holiday break authorities will estimate "thirty-five hundred cars an hour are pouring *out* of the state through the Kittery tollbooths."

Whether they're the same thirty-five hundred cars each time, nobody seems to know. Very few cars pour in or out over Washington's Birthday weekend.

At various points along the first seventy-five to a hundred miles of I-95, the vacationers peel off onto narrower highways—then secondary roads, the landscape dotted with signs like:

PIZZAS
WINE
VIDEOS

or

COLD BEER
VIDEOS
LIVE BAIT

They'll see an ever-increasing number of shops specializing in souvenirs, stained glass, hobby kits, or jewelry; crafts of all kinds. Along with speed limits, the roads of Maine, like its waterways, should today provide small-craft warnings.

Earlier, at Hobie's Store in the village, I had picked up a copy of the local weekly and the day's mail. Included with the latter was a short manuscript titled "Prologue," that I couldn't make much of anything out of, and an accompanying note from my son:

Dear Dad,
You've probably read the press releases announcing that I'm writing a book. It's to be a series of reminiscences about growing up as a son of somebody famous. I envision that it'll be real gutsy stuff—the inside story, no-holds-barred sort of thing. But told with great love and understanding. I feel privileged to have this chance to express myself so early in my career, Dad. Golly, I guess you were nearly twice my age before they asked you to do a book!
There's only one hitch. Since there's never been a tell-all biography by a kid about his parent or loved one

while the parent or loved one is still around to make trouble, the publisher says you've got to have a chance to respond, which shouldn't be too difficult.

Besides, it'll give you something to do up there! It'll also solve the publisher's concern over "legal complications from my accusations," whatever that means. Ha ha.

Enclosed is a copy of what I've done so far—kind of an introduction. Will be sending you chapters as I finish them. Probably will have the whole book done within a week or two, since I write fast, and this should be a piece of cake for us both. At least for me, ha ha.

Until next time, as you used to say, write if you get work!

Love,

Your son,

Chris

If there's one thing I don't need to be doing right now, just when I was going to concentrate on the festival, it's working on a book.

Besides, it's not my field. I've done a few articles over the years, mostly having to do with my hobbies. There was "Getting the Most Out of Your Lathe," "Lunch Meat—Discover Its Versatility," and "What's That Old Railroad Timetable Really Worth?" to name a few. But I don't really think I could expand these into book length.

Another hobby of mine, by the way, is old cars. I have a 1959 Ford Fairlane Galaxie in near mint condition, on which I've kept a meticulous log. It indicates just where I was, and what I was doing, each time the car passed a thousand-mile mark. (With 94,000 miles on her, maybe that could be a chapter in a book?)

I reread Chris's prologue and began to think perhaps the idea's not so bad, after all. What kind of book can my son, a young man whose chief claim to overnight fame is a routine called "The Japanese Spelling Bee," write? Answering his chapters might be just the chance to get a few things off my mind I've wanted to say for a long time.

He's talked himself into a book deal and needs my help, which he's seldom asked for before. He's never asked for much of anything really. He's always been a fast talker, but he's never had the gift of grab.

So why not? I'll go through the motions of rebutting his "accusations," and use the space to spice his prose with lighthearted thoughts and comment. A perfect way to use up a lot of non sequiturs I've collected over the years, and which heretofore had no place to go.

At my age, when I get what I think is a bright idea or a droll line comes to me, I jot it down. Otherwise I might forget it.

Like this note I scribbled on a cocktail napkin: "I'm at an age when, if I get a bright idea or a droll line comes to me, I write it down; otherwise I might forget it."

—Bob Elliott
Winship Harbor, Maine
May 26, 1988

NOTE TO MY READERS

The names of all persons appearing in my portions of this book are real, and the use of their names is intentional and okay by them. The places, events, and situations have been changed to make the story more palatable.

Birthday Hell

I GUESS YOU COULD SAY THAT LIFE with Daddy was a constant swirl of chaotic confusion, a muddled, mixed-up, jumbled existence . . . perhaps even upside-down, topsy-turvy, or helter-skelter. But I think even Daddy would have to agree that if nothing else, the life we led was always higgledy-piggledy. (Although at times it was also very discombobulated.)

I made my grand entrance into this world at the dawn of the decade of love: 1960. I appeared to be the perfect addition to the "Happy Bob Elliott Clan"—another boy. This would make it ten in a row for the beloved star. For my mother it was an uneventful birth, but for the hundreds of reporters, photographers, and gushing Bob Elliott fans who waited outside St. Vincent's Hospital for the official word, it was anything but uneventful. It was "sensational!"

Word spread fast—there was a new addition to "Bob's Boys," "The Elliott Scamps," "Bob's Thugs," and thousands of dollars exchanged hands as bookies took bets on the name Bob would give his new arrival. Would I be another Bob, Jr.? That was most certainly the "sure bet." My nine older brothers were named Bob, Jr., Number One; Bob, Jr., Number Two; Number Three; Number Four; all the way up to Number Nine (with the exception of the twins, who were fifth in line and named Bob, Jr., Number Five, A and B.) At the time this numbering of one's name-sakes was a common practice, and it was widely accepted by those in high places, those who were famous, and those who had Truly Arrived.

Daddy had truly arrived many years before, and was still riding the crest of a wave of popularity that would roll through five decades and nine presidents before finally crashing violently on the craggy rocks of a shore called Loneliness and Despair. The "Daddy's world" that I was born into was a far cry from the man's roots in this country. The son of a first-generation Greek immigrant, living in Brookline, Massachusetts, he had to work hard to achieve fame and fortune, something he never let me forget, and yet he was never satisfied. He always wanted more. Still, the Gravy Train moved at high speeds for Daddy. It was more like a Gravy Metro-liner whisking him from an oppressed childhood and traveling at two hundred miles an hour along the steel tracks of show business to land him ahead of schedule at Amtrak's Boyhood Dream station. Bob Elliott was now a superstar.

When I entered his world, he was at his height. You couldn't turn on the radio without hearing his deep, manly baritone belting out a lilting, romantic lullaby. You couldn't go to the movies without seeing his rock-solid shoulders and receding hairline fill the screen, and you couldn't go to the supermarket without seeing his cherubic face emblazoned on the labels of Bob Elliott's Famous Salad Dressing, or Bob Elliott's Popcorn, Chewing Tobacco, and Turkey Franks. He monopolized the talk shows and gossip columns. His appearance could turn a boring party into an "event." He composed, he performed, he lifted weights, and he painted all the murals in the lobby of the RCA Building. He was King of Comedy, King of Drama, and *Teen-Beat*'s Hunk of the Month at age fifty-five. He was a legend who cast a long black shadow, and there, in its darkness, my nine brothers and I shivered our way through childhood, huddled together like polar-bear cubs in the Arctic cold.

The evening of my arrival was plagued by a torrential downpour. (Was this a sign?) Outside St. Vincent's Hospital, the damp crowd grew restless. Tiffs broke out, then some quarrels, then spats turned to squabbles and small skirmishes metamorphosed into full-blown fistfights until the National Guard was called in to assist local law enforcement in cooling down the tense situation.

Finally, the crush of upset fans got what they wanted: Bob Elliott in person. He appeared flanked on either side by the Elliott Thugs, cradling in his arms his newborn son. I looked less like a baby and more like an overgrown, pink raisin. Still, Daddy seemed genuinely proud, and he seized the opportunity to hold an impromptu press conference. Paparazzi popped their flashbulbs and the mass roared its approval as he lifted me up over his head and held me suspended in outer space like a sacrifice to his adoring throng.

"I bet you all think you know the name of this

one!" he sputtered with a twinkle in his eye. "Do you suppose it's another Bob, Jr.?" he said teasingly. The mob went berserk, and they began to chant in unison, "Number Ten! Number Ten! Number Ten!"

"No, no, you're all wrong", he said. "I've decided to name this one Chris," and dead silence fell upon the flock. Was this some sort of cruel trick? Was I to be branded an outcast within minutes of my own birth? Would Daddy ever consider me truly one of the "scamps"? Perhaps it, too, was a sign, a warning light, a first alert. But I've grown to believe that it was Daddy's way of distinguishing me from my brothers. Ironically, I would be the one Thug he would work hardest at molding into his own image. He had big plans for his youngest son. I wouldn't be just another face in the family portrait of Bob's Boys. I would become, in time, Daddy's Boy.

My memory begins at the age of five. The images flash in my brain like one of Daddy's old silent movies. Images of an opulent life-style, of an exciting and glamorous era, of Manhattan in the mid-1960s. The sidewalks literally sparked with electricity back then, If Hollywood boomed in the twenties and thirties, Manhattan surely blossomed in the sixties and seventies.

Fox Run (or the Hut, as Daddy nicknamed it) was our home. A huge, sprawling mansion on the Upper East Side, boasting a two-acre backyard and expansive views of Central Park. It was, in fact, anything but a hut. It was a massive display of wealth and superstar status. The home still stands today, although no one lives there anymore. It now serves as Manhattan's Metropolitan Museum of Art. I often stroll up Fifth Avenue and sit in the American Stanhope Hotel's outdoor café sipping a cocktail while I gaze across the street at the Hut. What memories fill that house! What ghostly voices from my past echo in its halls! What a delicious Rob Roy they mix at the Stanhope! (And I can have all I want because I'm *not an alcoholic*!)

The museum people have done a marvelous job maintaining the exterior of the Hut. Although the pink stucco has long since been sanded off, the monstrous Corinthian columns still grace the front entrance, and the imposing stone steps that lead to it still seem to scream in a shrill, high-pitched voice, "If you're not a Vanderbilt or a Rockefeller, or if you have not 'truly arrived,' then get the hell out! We don't want you here!" Of course, the inside was gutted to make room for all the artifacts it now houses. But, oh, it was magnificent in its heyday!

When Daddy first bought Fox Run, he imported all the best Italian, French, Greek, and British designers and spared no expense on the palace's lavish interior decor. The marble floor of the main hall was blanketed in the most luxurious, thick, yellow wall-to-wall shag. The cold stone walls were bedecked in fake brick, and he insisted that bamboo roll-up blinds be the standard window treatment throughout. It was a fairy-tale world. There were two hundred and fifty rooms in the Hut. There were so many places to hide and play that you could leave reality behind and exist solely in the fantasy world of the Elliott Kingdom.

One of Daddy's favorite rooms was called the Beam Room. It was devoted entirely to his hideous collection of Beam whiskey bottles. I don't know how many he had, thousands probably, all arranged alphabetically on glass shelves. I thought the bottles were extremely ugly. How could a man with such good taste collect Beam bottles? I thought to myself. Yet I had never had the heart or guts to let him know how I truly felt.

I can remember often waking in the middle of the night to the strong aroma of Mum deodorant that wafted into my bedroom whenever Daddy passed by. Sometimes I'd follow the scent, and it always led me to the same place: the Beam Room. There he would be sitting, silently polishing the bottle shaped like a locomotive, or admiring the one celebrating gorillas, or gingerly caressing the one commemorating the Indy 500. He seemed the most at peace in the Beam Room. Perhaps it was his sanctuary—from the business, from the crowds of screaming teenage girls.

Once, when Daddy came home late from location shooting on *The Apple Dumpling Gang*, I followed the Mum trail into the Beam Room and sat with him amid his unsightly accumulation of bottles. There was a breeze in the room and the whistling wind made it difficult to hear what he was saying. He spoke softly, and I struggled to catch the words. He talked about how difficult life had been for him and how hard he'd had to work, and about not understanding a recent episode of *Gilligan's Island*. He was withdrawn and human, not the superstar anymore. I know I didn't grasp the subtleties of what he was trying to convey. I only know that the next words I heard rang out loud and clear and wrenched my guts like someone had split me open and taken a five-speed electric eggbeater to my intestines.

"One day when you have your own place," he said, "I want you to have my Beam bottle collection, Chris." I went back to my bedroom thoroughly depressed.

Besides the Beam Room, there was the Blue Room, the Green Room, the Flared Pants Room, and the Egyptian Room—which happens to be the only room the museum people left intact, thank God for that!

And so I was delivered into the hands of Manhattan royalty. We were an upscale version of the ideal American Family. We were the rosy-cheeked Norman Rockwell household, except we wore top hats and tails and fine lace. My early years passed semi-smoothly, and I adjusted quickly to our large home, our large family, and our larger-than-life Daddy. He was always busy, always working on a new project, and always filled with vim and vigor. Between 1961 and 1964, he starred in twelve films, wrote three novels, and appeared as the Tree in a children's production of *The Phantom Tollbooth*. Yet Daddy always found the time to take my brothers and me sailing, or horseback riding, or for long walks down to Riverside Park where we'd sit awhile and drop our lines into the murky Hudson and fish for eels. Just about every night the Elliott Tribe gathered around the great gold harp and listened to Daddy pluck away, and then there was the "horsing around." Daddy loved to "horse around." My brothers loved to "horse around," and I loved to "horse around." We were all experts at "horsing around." The "horse-around" hour always followed the Harp Concerts and could often escalate into major roughhousing that would leave the Hut in a shambles and my mother enraged.

She was not a "horsing-around" advocate. But this was all part of Daddy's image. SUPERSTAR MANAGES TO HAVE IT ALL! hailed a *Variety* headline. STAR OF STAGE AND SCREEN HEADS LOVING FAMILY, read *The Hollywood Reporter,* and *Life* magazine ran a ten-page profile applauding Daddy's "excellent parenting techniques."

It wasn't all public relations. He *was* a good parent. We learned strict manners early on. We all knew just what to say and how to behave when invited guests were in the house. We knew how to smile cutely at a bigwig Hollywood producer, or how to charm the pants off some Broadway angel, and how to curtsy properly for Manhattan royalty. Daddy never spanked us. He could be stern with us when he wanted to be, but there were never any red butts in our house. Daddy ruled solely through intimidation. Still, there was always a feeling of unrest hanging ominously in the great hall of the Hut. By the age of two I realized that the Elliott Clan was less Bob's Boys, and more Bob's Clones. He wanted all his sons to be like him, but I actually think he wanted me to *be* him. Does that make sense? No, that made no sense at all. (Sorry.)

As I grew out of the stroller and into a pair of sneakers, I took a more active role in the "horse-around" hour, and felt at ease being a celebrity's son. Life was good. It wasn't until things in Daddy's career began to change course that life in the Elliott household deteriorated.

My brothers and I all attended a very exclusive private school on Sixty-eighth and Lexington. It was called the Herbert School, and Daddy had been attracted, I suppose, by the progressive curriculum it offered. I, however, never felt at ease at Herbert. The school pushed artistic and spiritual growth over academic achievement. By third grade, most kids could see their own auras, but few of them could add or subtract.

The method of learning was based on the teachings of its founder, Wulfgang Herbert, a lesser-known German philosopher and hatmaker of the late eighteenth century. Herbert didn't believe in the right angle. In fact, he hated the right angle. "The thing is the violent intersection of two straight lines," he wrote, "and I'm damned if I can find a right angle anywhere in nature!" I think he's right about that, but it's no reason to hate the thing. He also felt that since there were no right angles in nature, there should be no right angles in anything man-made, including architecture. Every attempt at constructing a Herbert school without right angles met with disaster before the school could be completed, and so classes were held outside, literally on Sixty-eighth and Lexington.

My brothers fared well at Herbert, but I spent more time trying to poke holes in Wulfgang's theories than listening to teachers in class. I was often involved in street brawls with my classmates, and Daddy was routinely summoned to the corner coffee shop for conferences with my principal. Oddly enough, Daddy never reprimanded me for my behavior. If anything, he seemed to be reliving his childhood through me. As time wore on, I began to fit in at Herbert. I made a few friends and I did all the things kids are supposed to do: I played ball, drank cartons of warm milk, and attended birthday parties. I must say I went to some fun birthday parties at Herbert, but no parent could ever come close to producing the kind of birthday extravaganzas that Daddy mounted for my brothers and me.

Daddy loved our birthday parties. He loved to plan them weeks in advance and orchestrate them down to every last detail. He seemed to take extra pains in planning my birthday parties in particular. From the time I was born, my parties had become more and more elaborate each year. They grew from small gatherings of schoolmates to gigantic multimedia events covered by all three networks. In retrospect, the Manhattan birthday parties were really more for the adults than for the children. Although all my birthdays were special, one stands out. It was my sixth birthday, and Daddy pulled out all the stops.

I was always a very shy little boy. I was scared of clowns, and I retreated violently from anything that smacked of "audience participation." At a party, if a magician pulled me out of the group as his volunteer assistant, my body would immediately stiffen like a plank of wood and my scalp would foam up with hot sweat. Anything like a sing-along would elicit the same reaction. I remember needing oxygen at Macy's after meeting Santa Claus, and once I told Ronald McDonald that I wished he was dead. So, all in all, I was not a party boy, and no one knew this better than Daddy.

Still, my sixth birthday was to be bigger and better than any before. Daddy filled our backyard with

every conceivable form of audience participation
known to man. There were clowns, mimes, jugglers,
puppet shows, magicians, dancers—all eager to in-
volve me in their acts. There were fashion shows and
wrestling matches; and Graham Kerr, the Galloping
Gourmet, gave a cooking demonstration. It was
everything I hated.

I was allowed to invite only two of my classmates;
the rest of the invitations went out to Daddy's
friends. Among those who attended were Dick
Cavett, Al Hirschfeld, and Jerry Vale. Not the most
exciting group of playmates for a six-year-old kid.
Dick Cavett bent my ear for an hour about peanut
butter. But for my dad, the party was a big success.
As usual, the press was invited. The television networks set up their anchor booths around the yard,
and the Happy Elliott Clan public-relations machine
shifted into high gear. Music filled the backyard; it
was Steve Allen on the grand piano, Charles Kuralt
wrestled Andy Rooney shirtless, and Art Buchwald
rode the giant trained pig. At lunch the big table was
set, and I sat at the head of it. We ate bean-and-bacon
soup and filet mignon, blood-rare as usual, and the
photographers snapped their shots of the privileged
life of which the world was so envious.

After lunch we assembled in the Hut's game room
for the opening of the birthday presents; Bob, Jrs.,
One through Nine, all chipped in and bought me the
Broadway cast album to *Gypsy*—I still don't know
why.

"It's in high fidelity!" said Bob, Jr., Number One,
and then Number Two chirped in with, "You won't
hear any hissing!" I feigned appreciation. Each of

Daddy's friends gave me a copy of their own auto-biographies and my two invited classmates accidentally duplicated their gifts—Operation by Milton Bradley. Then it was time to open Daddy's present to me.

The box was a huge square, five feet by five, and wrapped in festive, bright-colored paper. My eyes popped out when I saw it. I tore madly at the paper and opened the box, but curiously there was another box inside. It was slightly smaller and wrapped similarly to the first one. I tore open this box, and again there was a slightly smaller box concealed within. Again I opened the box, and again there was a smaller box. This pattern repeated itself long into the evening, as the boxes shrank smaller and smaller. Finally I reached what had to be the last box. It was tiny. I thought to myself, "This has to be something good. Maybe it's one big diamond, or the keys to a cool electric car, or maybe a check for a thousand dollars." Something wonderful had to be in that box. Slowly I tore off the wrapping paper. I opened the box and peered inside; all I could see was a piece of paper folded a hundred times. I pulled the note out, unfolded it, and read out loud: "To Daddy's boy, Happy sixth birthday, my son. Use this in good health! Fondly, your father, Bob Elliott."

It was a touching moment, and Daddy looked a bit embarrassed. I peered back into the box to see what I would "use in good health." Inside was an itsy-bitsy comb no more than an inch long.

"What is it?" I inquired, holding the thing up. Everyone in the room including Daddy laughed. Then Daddy said, "Well, what do you think it is, son? It's a mustache comb!"

Birthday Hell

The room exploded in applause. Daddy hugged me. "I hope you like it," he said.

"Oh, sure, Dad, it's great, thanks a lot!" I hugged him back and everyone went to eat cake. I was then—and I am now—more baffled by the mustache comb than disappointed.

Later that evening, something else happened that was pretty odd. After all the guests had gone home, Daddy walked me down to the Movie House, a small building by the pool where Daddy viewed his movies.

"You're now six years old, Christopher," he spoke sternly while he squeezed my shoulder "It is time you became a man."

He led me into the viewing room and left me in the pitch-black darkness. After a moment I heard the whirring sound of the projector starting up behind me, and before I knew it, I was face-to-face with *Psycho*, starring Anthony Perkins. I was forced to watch the film three times in a row before the door to the viewing room reopened and Daddy appeared. We walked together up the hill to the Hut.

"I hope you understand why I did that," he said as we made our way up the stone walk.

"Sure, Dad, of course I understand, what d'ya think, I'm dumb or something?"

He smiled at me. "That's a good Daddy's boy. Now you run along to bed—and happy birthday and pleasant dreams!"

I didn't have pleasant dreams at all that night. I had nightmares of kitchen knives slashing at shower curtains, of old gray-haired ladies, of blood and guts, and of Art Buchwald riding the giant trained pig. Yet perhaps Daddy's lesson meant something, after all.

Maybe my birthday hell would play some part in building my character.

Still later that night, with my mind lost in the parking lot of the Bates Motel, my nostrils filled with the familiar Mum aroma. I woke immediately, and there, standing in my doorway, was Daddy. He was naked except for a pair of inflatable undershorts. (The undershorts were something he had seen advertised on television. Supposedly, if you wore them to bed, you could lose weight in your sleep.) He stood swaying in the doorway for an eternity. Then, in a hushed voice, almost a whisper, he implored: "If you eat spaghetti, please watch out for the bay leaves!"

He turned and was gone as suddenly as he had appeared.

My sixth birthday was, in a way, like so many other days to come. Days that twirled crazily around the swirl of confusion into which Daddy was slowly spiraling down. He was a supernova falling from the universe, and he was going to take me with him. If my sixth birthday should stand out for any reason, it should be that it marked the beginning—the beginning of a changed relationship between Daddy and me. I still don't know what he meant, standing in my doorway talking about spaghetti. Was he trying to control my mind? Was he sleepwalking? Or was he just plain nuts? The one thing I knew for sure was that the road ahead would be a bumpy one and that I would have to keep a sharp lookout for all the "bay leaves" that were headed my way.

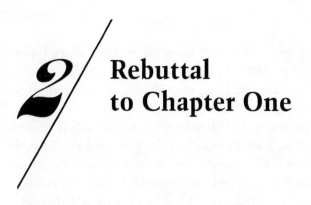

Rebuttal
to Chapter One

CHRIS WAS BORN THE YEAR ARTHUR
Godfrey recorded "Teterboro Tower."

I begin with this, not because it was such a monumental event (Arthur's recording, I mean—not the birth of my son), but because over the years I've developed the habit of associating happenings with dates I want to remember.

This probably stems from my early years as a disc jockey when I put in long hours reading commercials, delivering news, and mixing small talk with patter about the records I spun.

Thus I remember that Bing Crosby went into a studio on January 27, 1942, with John Scott Trotter and his orchestra, and recorded "I Don't Want to Walk Without You" from the Paramount Picture *Sweater Girl*. It was the same day I got my draft notice for service in World War II.

I also remember that Helen Forrest, with Harry James's Band, cut her smash record "I've Heard That Song Before" on July 31, 1944, although by that time I was overseas and don't have anything in particular to associate with that bit of musical minutia.

Daddy's Boy

(Who among you will remember, fifty years from now, that in 1988 *Rolling Stone* chose "Walk Away Renee" by Left Banke as one of "the 100 best singles of the past quarter century"?)

Anyway, in his first few years, Chris made it abundantly clear that he was a different kind of child. I sensed this when, by the age of four, he was begging me to buy him Jenny Lind records. I tried to get him interested in Yma Sumac, but it was a futile attempt.

By the time he was six or seven, he had developed an interest in Enrico Caruso—for what reason we never did figure out—and he would save up his weekly fifty-cent allowances until he had enough for another Caruso record. This bullheaded determination continued well into his adult years, by which time he had amassed a Caruso collection numbering into the thousands.

He seemed blind to the fact that Caruso records had been issued in such great numbers and were owned by so many people, that even if he did possess one of the largest collections in the world, the entire thing was only worth around six dollars and seventy-five cents.

Add to this the fact that the boy didn't have an ear for music—nor the slightest talent for it—and you begin to realize Chris was, indeed, a different kind of child.

What you've read so far is the way I'd been planning to start my story. But that was before today's mail arrived, and with it, the pages of Chris's first chapter. Right away I could see that spending my time on the Festival idea would be much more profitable than trying to answer his ridiculous charges, as sure as my name isn't John Cougar Mellencamp.

I don't know what Chris is talking about. He doesn't have nine brothers. He has three sisters and one brother. We did not live in the Metropolitan Museum of Art, and I have never in my life had the pleasure of meeting Mr. Jerry Vale, although I would not turn down such an opportunity if it presented itself. Do my lawyers actually think people are going to take this book seriously?

I began to ponder fresh ways to begin my chapter, at the same time tossing around ideas for the Finnan Haddie Festival which, by rights, should be receiving my full attention. The sun warmed the deck as I relaxed in one of the creaking Adirondack chairs scattered across it, sipping coffee from a mug given me years ago by someone on the New York *Herald Tribune*. Scanning what passed for headlines on the front page of the local weekly I'd picked up with the mail, I thought there must be an ironic connection between them and the message on the side of the mug: "Who Says a Good Newspaper Has to Be Dull?"

A friend of mine, Bob Cooke, was an ace sportswriter on the *Trib* until he retired to Florida. On days like this he was fond of quoting a fellow columnist, Bob Sylvester. Sylvester supposedly heard a Miamian say "It's such a beautiful day, I think I'll take the TV out on the porch!"

Suddenly it occurred to me I might get some encouragement re the Festival idea from my neighbor, Daryll Dexter. He always seems to have a knack for getting to the nitty-gritty of a problem and coming up with suggestions that make you feel sheepish for not having thought of them yourself.

I hopped in the Ford and drove the short distance out onto the point where Daryll and his wife, Darla, live. They've created a home out of a lighthouse decommissioned in 1981 when a larger, more visible tower was erected on a higher elevation a half mile away.

Daryll is a former computer programmer for a major data-processing engineering systems corporation in the East, who now works part-time as a substitute teacher in Portland. His hobbies are fishing and doing impressions of Rich Little. His earnings so far this year amount to a total of one hundred and thirteen thousand dollars.

He looks a lot like the Frugal Gourmet.

He's the kind of guy who always seems to have the inside track on everything. Like their home, which is the envy of everyone around here. He'd heard about the property being up for auction by the government, and ended up making the winning bid. Then he and Darla went about a remodeling job that would make Bob Vila and Norm Abrams proud.

Along with this, Daryll's a big television fan, especially a fan of game shows, and as a result he's a walking compendium of odd and offbeat information. In short, someone I enjoyed exchanging trivia with.

I parked in the driveway at the foot of the light and was greeted by his dog, Vanna, a pointer.

"Haven't we got enough festivals already?" Daryll asked as soon as we were inside and I'd briefly outlined my idea.

Rebuttal to Chapter One

"Maybe," I replied, "but I think it might give the state a shot where it would do some good; create interest and extra revenue. Summer folks are tired of the same old Broiler Festival in Belfast, and the Yarmouth Clam Festival, and even the Lobster Festival in Rockland."

"You'll have a hell of a time selling the idea to Augusta," he said. "Only time I beat the government was when I bid for this lighthouse and got it. Otherwise they're a bunch of . . ."

Daryll is like that, always assuming an adversarial position against the system. He'll often void where prohibited.

"I still marvel at what you've done with this place," I said, glancing around appreciatively.

"The bidding was fast and furious, I'll tell you," Darla interjected as she handed me a cup of coffee.

"Price went up faster than the rates at a New York City parking garage," Daryll added. "But you know," he continued in a more serious vein, "these places are becoming scarcer and scarcer. There are only a dozen or so manned lighthouses left in this country—all of 'em along this coast. And next year they'll take the last one out of service. Oh, we'll have the lights, of course, and the foghorns, but there won't be any lighthouse keepers anymore."

"I read somewhere that the very first one was in Boston Harbor," I said, warming to the subject. "On Little Brewster Island, was that it?"

"Yes, built in 1716," Daryll replied. "Portland Head Light down the coast here was built in 1791. It's one of the oldest in the East. Lighthouses didn't get out to the West Coast until almost a hundred years later, around the time of the Gold Rush. Alcatraz Island Lighthouse was the first out there, built in 1854. Then came the one at Point Loma, south of San Diego, in 1855. It's part of the Cabrillo National Monument there."

"You know why lighthouses are usually white?" asked Darla.

"So they'll stand out against the sky, I guess," I answered.

"Exactly," said Daryll.

"And speaking of that," I said, "I've always wondered how they paint those black-and-white spiral stripes around the sides of the Cape Hatteras Lighthouse—and others, too—and get them exactly the right distance apart all the way down."

"There's a wild spot!" Daryll exclaimed. "It's where the warm Gulf Stream, flowing north at about four knots, veers in close to shore. It made an inviting sea-lane for the Spanish treasure fleets coming from the mines in Mexico and Central America on their way back to Europe.

"But at Diamond Shoals, the inshore current and the jutting fingers of shifting sand forced over five hundred southbound ships of all nations to founder, and the whole area earned its reputation as the Graveyard of the Atlantic.

"Congress recognized the danger to shipping and authorized construction of the Hatteras Light in 1794. It took nearly ten years to build, but finally, in 1803—October, to be specific—the light 'was raised,' its lamp fueled by sperm-whale oil.

"But there were complaints," he continued, "that the small lamp didn't adequately penetrate the darkness beyond the shoals, and the light was often out for days when storms broke the windows of the tower.

"In the 1850s, the tower was raised to more than a hundred and fifty feet and a new light installed, improving things considerably. Then, in 1861, during the Civil War, the tower suffered extensive damage, and rather than repair it, Congress decided to build a new Cape Hatteras Light six hundred feet north of the original tower to escape the danger of erosion. The old tower was eventually destroyed and the present one equipped with a rotating electric beacon in 1972.

"In clear weather the beam can be seen twenty miles away, and some reports indicate it's been observed as far as fifty miles at sea.

"But, hey! I must be sounding like those ponderous pseudo-philosophical ramblings Hugh Hefner used to go on," said Daryll.

"Not at all," I replied, in a manner not like me. "I've always wondered how they paint—"

"Most everybody thinks lighthouse keepers were always men," Daryll went on, "but the old Point Fermin light in San Pedro, California, was originally kept by two women, the Smith sisters, who moved there in 1874, thinking the climate would be healthy. It's run now as a bed and breakfast place, I think.

"I don't know whether I mentioned that Hatteras Light is the tallest in the United States. It's 208 feet from the base to the top of the roof, and the light is 191 feet above the mean high-water mark. There are 268 steps from the ground to the light, and the whole thing cost $150,000 in 1870."

"Oh," I said.

"There are 1,250,000 bricks in her."

"Uh-huh," I commented.

Darla made a nervous throat-clearing sound.

"I was wondering about—"

"Oh, yes, the stripes," said Daryll. "I wondered about that myself, so I looked into the matter. Turns out they wrapped two ropes an equal space apart down and around the outside of the lighthouse, and that gave them the pattern for painting."

"I should have thought of that myself," I said sheepishly. Then, sensing I'd learned all I needed to learn this visit, and not wishing to overstay my welcome, I prepared to head home.

"The stripes were first painted on in 1806, three years after the lighthouse was built, and they repaint them every seven to ten years, I'm told," Daryll added.

By now I'd reached the Ford and, with thanks for the coffee, I started the engine.

"Be seeing you soon," I called to Daryll and Darla, who stood in the doorway of their home. "Have fun, you two!"

"You two too," Darla shouted, in an apparent reference to my wife and me, as I drove away.

3 / "No More Gold-Toe Socks!"

NO MATTER HOW MANY BAY LEAVES I plucked from the spaghetti sauce of my life, there was always a handful of sneaky ones that managed to slip by, and inevitably I would find myself munching down on their bitterness and struggling unsuccessfully to mask my total embarrassment.

In a galaxy of celebrities, Bob Elliott shined brighter and flew higher than all the other stars combined, but on a sixth-grade field trip to the Hayden Planetarium I learned that even big, bright stars can plummet violently from the universe. (Later, in my troubled teens, I would return to the planetarium, but they were doing a laser show to Pink Floyd music and it made me dizzy.) Daddy's career had been speeding along on a newly paved highway, overtaking other careers that perhaps were running out of gas. But a traffic jam was around the next turn. He would suddenly find himself bumper to bumper, inching along ever so slowly, and he would have to switch off the air-conditioning to save the engine from overheating. He may have seen it coming, but I doubt it. If he had foreseen the backup, he would have taken Exit 3, which was the scenic route and would have bypassed the clogged area completely. So I'm sure he was not aware of the heavy traffic he was approaching, and I know I certainly wasn't. I had problems of my own to deal with.

I was the nine-year-old son of a celebrity, and every day I was, in appearance, becoming more and more like the legend. I was being molded into a miniature Bob Elliott, with every last detail intricately scaled down. Every subtlety, every nuance that made up my father was to be duplicated in me. Dance instructors, acting coaches, and speech therapists were hired to teach me to walk, talk, and act like the great Bob Elliott. Every article of clothing in his wardrobe was reproduced in my size. This work was done by a group of disgruntled wetbacks who labored long hours and for very little pay in the stuffy sweat shops that Daddy ran in the north wing of the Hut. Thousands of outfits were duplicated for me.

The day's attire was usually simple. It consisted of flared gray slacks; snappy blue sport coat; oxford shirt and ascot; knee-high black Gold-Toe socks; and, of course, the buckwhite wooden shoes that by now had become Daddy's familiar trademark. There were, however, those days when Daddy felt a little extra frisky, and so we would don our French sailor outfits, and on extremely bright or sunny days we paraded about in our colorful Bella Abzug floppy hats.

The "dressing alike" became a source of much tension between my father and me. None of my brothers were subjected to this humiliation, and I felt it unfair. But the more I complained, the more determined and obsessed he became.

By this time Daddy's thick mane of golden curls had all but disappeared. His hairline had receded back almost out of sight, revealing his billiard-ball cranium. I know the contrast between his egghead and my towhead bothered him greatly. I overheard him bellowing to my mother late one night, "He's just got *too much hair*! I mean, look at him and look at me, it's too damn disconcerting!" . . . and I heard my mother trying to comfort him. "I know, dear, I know." Ultimately, and like everything else in our lives, Daddy would find a solution to the problem. A makeup man was hired and I was fitted with a special latex "bald-head" wig. I hated the bald wig. The damn thing was much too tight and I felt silly in it. At Herbert, the kids were ruthless. "Chrome-Dome!", "Skin-Head!", and "Otto Preminger!" were the least offensive nicknames hurled my way.

Daddy couldn't walk down the street without being screamed at, and I couldn't walk down the street without being stared at. I became acutely paranoid. Everyone was staring at me, I knew it. Eyes, eyes everywhere. Even dogs and cats looked at me sideways, and I found myself becoming aggressively hostile to pigeons. "What are you looking at?"; "Why don't you just go fly into a brick wall!"; "All you are is a rat with wings!" Luckily for me, the application of the bald cap took three hours, and Daddy became annoyed when I was consistently late for appointments. So eventually the wig was abandoned and Mommy simply shaved my hairline back to match Daddy's.

Daddy's Boy

In 1969, a flashing light and sign on the interstate warned, SLOW FOR TRAFFIC UP AHEAD, and Daddy was forced to let up on the accelerator of his career. The entertainment industry heralded the beginning of a new era. In the movies, the big, strong, macho superheroes like Daddy were being overlooked by audiences who preferred the more gentle antihero types; the Butch Cassidys and the Midnight Cowboys. In the world of music, Daddy maintained a loyal following, although he found himself forced to cover hits by Cream and Jefferson Airplane. On the Broadway stage, with the exception of *Godspell* (which Daddy was not right for), musical comedy died, and he was losing dramatic roles to newcomers Al Pacino and Robert DeNiro. It seemed the ethnic look was in and Norman Rockwell was out. To his credit, Daddy worked hard to keep up with the changing times. He wore "funky, groovy" shirts and safari jackets, let his sideburns go untrimmed, and grew the remaining wisps of his hair down to shoulder length. Unfortunately his efforts were only rewarded with a small part in *Night of the Living Dead*. Still, there was always his weekly radio address, the *Singalong with Bob Hour* on ABC, and the construction of Bob's Big Towers (a giant office complex to be built in lower Manhattan). But the fact remained, Bob Elliott needed a hit and he needed it soon.

Things got worse. Work began to fall off, the offers stopped coming in, and Daddy withdrew from the world. Fame was giving him a lashing he would never forget. Although my emotions were confused, I know I felt sympathy for the man. Still, no matter how hard the hard times were, I was not going to allow him to take away my measly fifty-dollar-a-week allowance.

He spent most of his days in the Bad Paintings on Velvet Room, going over his options and holding strategy meetings with his longtime manager, Sid Smiley. Together they worked late into the night, trying to map out the first of many comebacks for Daddy, and Sid always kept an optimistic attitude. He was always around the house, even in good times; so much so, in fact, that the clan had taken to calling him Uncle Sid, although he was of no relation.

Uncle Sid was a short, nervous fellow, already in his late eighties. His appearance was slovenly. His shirttails hung out, and his one heavy tweed suit looked as though a coal miner had worn it to work. Daddy overlooked this slobbery, I suppose, because of their lifelong relationship. He certainly wouldn't have tolerated any of the Scamps being ill-kempt. Daddy and Uncle Sid had met ages before on the dim stages of vaudeville. Back then, Sid was a performer himself; known as The Great Inhaler. His act consisted of chewing and swallowing lit cigars, broken glass, razor blades, light bulbs, keys, and anything his audience challenged him with. He was a big hit, on his way to becoming a big star, when he gave it all up to handle the career of a promising young acrobat named Bobby Elliott. Uncle Sid's days of swallowing dangerous objects were over, but they had taken their toll. He wheezed heavily when he breathed and when he spoke; he hummed annoyingly after each sentence. But he was a loyal friend to Daddy, and he was fun to have around the house; and yes, my brothers and I could still coax him into swallowing the odd fish hook every now and then.

I bring up Sid for many reasons, but mainly because it was Sid who, in this Dark Age of Daddy's career, planted a seed in my ten-year-old soul. It was a dream I had never dared to dream; a vision, though still out of focus, that I would hold in my heart forever. It was a vision of the distant future, and, like Nostradamus, Uncle Sid was able to see that future, and he described it to me one afternoon.

It was late and my brothers and I were out in front of the Hut trying to play a game of touch football with some neighborhood kids.

It was difficult to play out front, not because of the concrete sidewalk but because of the special harnesses we were forced to wear. Each harness was personally monogrammed. It consisted of heavy canvas shoulder straps that crisscrossed in the front and the back and were sewn to a canvas belt worn at the waist. Connected to the belt was a canvas strap about a hundred feet long; that, in turn, was securely attached to one of the giant Corinthian columns decorating the Hut's front entrance. The hundred-foot strap did not give us much area to run and play in before being yanked back, and you can imagine how difficult a game of touch football would be. But Daddy felt that the harnesses were a necessary precaution in the Big City. He called them our Play Safes, but in actuality they were nothing more than another humiliation we had no choice but to bear. The Elliott Boys would always forfeit their games of touch football. Inevitably, by the game's first play, the ten long straps would become tangled and intertwined, forming a complex web of canvas that could take up to an hour to unknot.

We had just finished when Uncle Sid appeared. He asked my brothers to go into the house. He wanted to talk to me alone, and they obliged him. "Let's you and me take a walk, ummmmmm," he said, and we strolled south on Fifth Avenue.

There was something important on his mind, I could tell. "You know your father is going through a tough time," he wheezed out.

"You're telling me!" I replied, and with that Sid let out a long hacking cough. "Are you all right, Uncle Sid?" I asked.

"I'm fine," he said. "Something went down the wrong pipe at lunch, that's all."

We continued our walk and Sid spoke his mind. "What I'm trying to say, young Chris, is that there will come a time when your daddy will have to pass the torch, ummmmmmm. A time when you'll have to carry on in his tradition, ummmmmmmmmm. A time when you'll have to step into the old man's shoes, ummmmmm." We stopped walking. He looked me straight in the eye and said, "I just want you to know that when that time comes, I would like to be your manager, ummmmmmm."

It immediately occurred to me that if I ever decided to go into show business, it certainly wouldn't be till after college, about fifteen years down the line, and by then Uncle Sid would be 103 years old. But still, I thanked him politely and told him I'd keep him in mind.

As we continued our stroll Sid continued to sell

himself. "I mention it only because I feel like I've done a good job for your daddy, ummmmmmmm. And I think I could do the same for you, ummmmmmmm." Suddenly I was pulled violently from behind and slammed facedown on the hard concrete sidewalk. I had forgotten I was still attached to my Play Safe, and the long umbilical cord had run out of slack.

My surprise pratfall sent Uncle Sid into another coughing fit worse than the first. He made a strange gurgling sound, took a deep breath, and as he exhaled, an unidentified flying object cannonballed out of his mouth and landed in his cupped hands. It was a shot glass, and he held it up to his eye, examining the stenciled lettering on it. "Altantic City, 1918," he read, only slightly amused. "Here, you keep this as a good-luck charm." He handed me the wet shot glass and went to hail a cab. "Don't forget what we talked about!" he shouted. "Fame can be yours, too, my son, ummmmmmmm!" And with that he was off.

The seed had been planted. "Fame can be yours too." Those words echoed in my brain and resounded off the inside of my skull like a giant bell. One day Daddy's Boy might be famous, might be a star, might be Manhattan Royalty. Oh, it seemed so impossible. Fame was Daddy's treasure; it wasn't going to be handed to me like his lousy Beam bottle collection. I knew it was too early for me to make any decisions, and I tried to put the whole idea out of my head.

On the home front, life for the happy Elliott Clan ground to a halt. With his career stalled on the highway of fame and fortune, Daddy took to wandering the great halls of the Hut, muttering to himself and desperately trying to come up with that one move that would put him back on top. Never was the dichotomy greater between the Bob Elliott perceived by his loyal fans and the Bob Elliott who floated aimlessly through the Hut. To his public he was still a shining star. It didn't matter that he wasn't on the big screen or the radio airwaves or the TV tube; to them he was a legend granted eternal life. But this was not enough for Daddy. He felt frustrated, lost, and alone. Unfortunately he seemed to vent most of this frustration on his youngest son, the one most like him.

I began to believe that everything he did, everything he said, every look that creased his poker face, had but one purpose, and that purpose was to bug the bejesus out of me. Little things began to add up. I despised Sundays. Sundays meant the end of the weekend and school the next day. I would actually get a nauseous feeling in my stomach when I heard the ticking theme to *60 Minutes*. It signaled the countdown to bedtime. Somehow I knew Daddy secretly reveled in my nausea regarding *60 Minutes*. I hated eating first thing in the morning, and yet every day I was required to down a glass of banana-flavored Carnation Instant Breakfast and could not leave the table until I had done so. I was sure Daddy enjoyed watching me choke down the chemical mixture. Any free time was filled with little chores, specially concocted by Daddy. Usually they were inane, humiliating tasks: perhaps sorting his pocket change or cutting up his old credit cards for shirt stays: or decanting his Hi-Karate after-shave into crystal goblets marked Aramis.

"Night raids" became commonplace. It would be two, maybe three in the morning, and suddenly the lights in my bedroom would blast on. I would rub the crust from my eyes and focus on Daddy in his inflatable undershorts, his face covered with Noxzema. He would run his index finger along the marble mantelpiece and check it for dust. Then he would open the flue to the fireplace and make sure I had swept the chimney before bed. Next he'd turn on my Sony TV set and play around with the color balance. Finally he'd go to my wardrobe closet and peruse my blue blazers, my oxford shirts, my Nehru jackets and dickies, my jodhpurs and breeches and my dhotis and flip-flops. Everything had to be in its place. Especially the hundred or so pair of black knee-high Gold-Toe socks.

He seemed particularly concerned about the care of the Gold-Toe socks. Of course, I had to wear them everywhere, including gym class and the beach; and in the evenings before bedtime, they were to be hung properly on nothing else but wire hangers. "After a day's wear, nothing but a wire hanger can put the buoyancy back in a Gold-Toe sock," he would say, and I would think to myself, "I'd like to put the buoyancy back in *your* socks, pal!"

Perhaps it was the strain of his faltering career that drove him to complete compulsion, but he became forever hooked on Gold-Toe socks. Not just the socks themselves but the *idea* of the socks. His obsession monopolized all his creative energies. He began to scribble notes about Gold-Toe socks on cocktail napkins. He drew up chart after chart tracing the history of Gold-Toe socks from Paleolithic times to the present. He sketched lovely, life-like renderings of Gold-Toe socks, and his office was filled with reams of treatments for short stories and novels, all about Gold-Toe socks: "The Gold-Toe Socks Murders," "The Life and Loves of the Gold-Toe Socks," "Pippi Longstocking and Her Gold-Toe Socks," and so on.

His preoccupation did not go unnoticed by those outside the family. Gradually the lavish dinner parties dwindled; the big stars and producers and directors stopped dropping in; eventually many of the servants sought employment elsewhere. Even old Uncle Sid would roll his eyes when Daddy would go off on long, boring war stories about Gold-Toe socks.

Then came the last straw. It was Christmas Eve 1970, and a television reporter named Jerry Dunphey had set up his cameras in our living room for another installment of *Jerry Visits*. This was supposed to be a visit with the happy Bob Elliott Clan. But here is the shocking transcript of Jerry's visit:

JERRY DUNPHEY

Good evening, America. It's Christmas Eve and I'm sitting in the tastefully decorated living room of the Crown Prince of Manhattan Royalty, one of our nation's greatest treasures: Mr. Bob Elliott. With us also this evening are those little devils, the Elliott Scamps, and they've graciously invited us to sip some eggnog and spend a few minutes of Christmas cheer with them on this very special evening. Bob, perhaps you could start by introducing the tribe? Would ya?

Daddy's Boy

BOB ELLIOTT

Sure, Jerry, I'd be happy to. Sitting to my left here are Bob, Jrs., One through Four. Standing behind me are Bob, Jrs., Six through Nine. On the floor are the twins, A and B, and to my right is my favorite son, Chris. And if I could, I'd just like to add that we're all wearing Gold-Toe socks.

JERRY

Well, that's very nice. Chris, are you excited about tomorrow?

CHRIS *(depressed)*

Why would you ask that?

JERRY

Why, it's Christmas! What do you boys hope Santa brings you tomorrow?

BOYS *(muttered all together)*

Gold-Toe socks . . . socks . . . yeah, more socks . . . yeah, we really need some socks.

BOB

That's right. You see, Jerry, the boys will receive hundreds of presents in the mail from my adoring fans, but all those gifts will be sent to those less fortunate. And my kids will be allowed to keep one present each tomorrow: a brand-new pair of beautiful, black, knee-high Gold-Toe socks, fifty-fifty blend!

"No More Gold-Toe Socks!"

JERRY

I see . . . um, well . . . ah, what's planned for this evening? I'm sure Christmas Eve must be extra-special in the Bob Elliott household.

BOB

Oh, it sure is, Jerry. First we'll invite the neighborhood children in to sing some Christmas carols. Then the boys will hang their old Gold-Toe socks on the chimney with care, then we'll all sit by the roaring fire and kick off our shoes and check each other's socks for lint balls, then later on we'll read out loud from Dickens's classic "Christmas Sock Story," then—

CHRIS *(standing up and shouting)*

That's it! That's the last straw! I have had it up to here with your stupid Gold-Toe socks! You're driving everyone in this family nuts! Gold-Toe socks this, Gold-Toe socks that! No more Gold-Toe socks! Get yourself some help, man! You've gone off the deep end in a bad way! Merry Christmas! (Chris storms out of the room.)

PAUSE.

JERRY *(stunned)*

We'll be right back.

It probably was not the best thing to do. The program was broadcast coast-to-coast that night, and for weeks afterward Daddy received hundreds of pairs of Gold-Toe socks in the mail from wackos who had seen the show. I had let my emotions get away from me. I was out of control. But in a strange way I felt a great release. I had finally stood up for myself and for my brothers. Unfortunately it did nothing to deter Daddy from continuing his pursuit of Gold-Toe socks. No, it was Uncle Sid who was our savior that Christmas.

Daddy was welding twenty-four hours a day on a giant, bronze sock statue, and the family was on the brink of implosion when Sid arrived with the good news. It seemed Hal Holbrook had taken ill and was forced to bow out of his one-man show as Bela Lugosi. The producers needed a replacement right away . . . and they wanted Bob Elliott. This was it; this was the break Daddy had been waiting for. This was the project that would lift him back into the stratosphere. It would be a one-year worldwide tour, kicking off first in London, then traveling through Europe, and then the United States. Daddy's prayers had been answered, and for the time being, all projects involving Gold-Toe socks were shelved.

I personally felt the show was a mixed blessing. I was happy to bid farewell to Daddy's sock obsession, but I was informed that I would be accompanying him to London and Europe. No one else would be along, just Daddy and me. Quite frankly, the prospect terrified me, but as with everything else, I had no say in the matter.

And so the traffic jam cleared and the engine in Daddy's career started back up without a glitch. Ahead was a long road, but it looked like easy driving. No one, not even Uncle Sid or Nostradamus, could really predict the future, and I maintained a hopeful but cautious outlook. As I packed my bags and readied myself for the long journey ahead, I couldn't stop thinking about Uncle Sid's words: "Fame can be yours, too, my son, ummmmmmm." Perhaps if I was to attain such heights as Daddy, I would have to start sooner than expected, and perhaps the trip to Europe would be a good training ground. Maybe I would learn something . . . some trick of the trade . . . Daddy's secret for success. The atmosphere seemed right.

I was filled with anticipation. For the first time in my life I began to feel like maybe I could be somebody too. But Bob Elliott's shadow was a long one, indeed, and I would soon learn that no matter how hard I tried to walk in his path without actually stepping in his footsteps, I would always be wearing his socks.

Rebuttal
to Chapter Three

I'VE GOT TO ADMIT IT. I MAY BE HAVing reservations about this inchoate book.

That's the first time I've ever had occasion to use the word *inchoate,* and this seemed like the right one. If Chris can throw in concupiscence, amentia, and lycanthropy, I can certainly use *inchoate.*

I'd like to work in oligopoly, oligopsony, and monopsony somehow, but I haven't been able to figure out a comfortable way. Unless I could contrive a situation where a character had occasion to say, "That, sir, is a monopsony—not an oligopsony!"

Maybe one of these days I'll spring a word like that on Chris while he's quietly listening to his Blaupunkt. (He doesn't really have a Blaupunkt—I just like to say the word.)

As I said, I was having reservations about this book. Maybe I'm a little skeptical about the feasibility of the whole idea. But then, I'm that way. I was skeptical when Stevie Wonder announced he might throw his hat into the ring for the 1992 Detroit mayoral race.

Actually, I found nothing particular in Chapter Three that called for an answer. Matter of fact, I found some of it amusing—even the part about socks.

It's obvious he's going to make a big thing out of this. I'd mention the brand myself, but I see no reason giving these sock makers a big plug and not getting paid for it. The golden days of payola (as wonderful as they were) are over; only the most naive performer would today participate in such scams.

On the other hand, having already dropped in the name Blaupunkt, I've shot down my own thesis on commercial integrity, so let's forget it.

As far as I can remember, Chris never wore socks at all. He wore shoes occasionally, but they were always Wallabees or Chucka Boots, and he never used laces. Once he came home wearing a pair of those ridiculous-looking Earth shoes, but I never held it against the kid.

We were well into the middle of June, experiencing some unseasonably wet weather, when my son's latest installment came. I guessed that his schedule had interfered with his plans for dashing out the book "in a week or two." As long as it was on the rainy and chilly side, I decided this a good chance to stay indoors and do some research for the festival.

Sad to say, I found very little anywhere on the subject of finnan haddie. I remembered the story I'd heard as a kid about the fisherman in Scotland who hung up his catch—mostly haddock, probably—in a wooden shack and that the shack caught fire one night. When he went out to inspect the damage next morning, he looked at the fish lying there, poked his finger into one of them, and—lo and behold!—discovered it had a wonderful taste. From then on finnan haddie was in.

But hardly enough in that to build a festival on.

The telephone rang, and Daryll interrupted my studies.

"There was something I think I forgot to mention when we had that interesting discussion the last time you were over here," he began, sounding nothing like they sound in Cabot Cove.

"Oh?" I said.

He went on. "Thirty-three years after that lighthouse on Little Brewster Island was built, they put one up in Newport, Rhode Island Harbor, and after that another in Nantucket Harbor—both before the one at Portland Head!"

"I finished that chapter, Daryll," I told him, and hung up, concluding our conversation.

I returned to my inchoate fish research.

5/ Our Trip on the *Andrea Doria*

THE SEA IS A CRUEL MISTRESS. IT can be our friend, but it can also be our enemy. It can serve us and yet it can enslave us. It may caress gently one moment, and in the next instant slap viciously. It is schizophrenic. It is out of its mind. It is completely insane. It is a crazed killer, a murderous psychopath, void of any socially redeeming qualities . . . and it is the scourge of the earth, roaming freely from one continent to the next, spreading disease and destruction, raping and pillaging our homes and our villages, and laying to waste everything in its evil path. It must be stopped. The sea knows not from right and wrong. it cannot distinguish between good and evil. It is like a child, undisciplined from birth, and in that way, Daddy was very much like the sea.

It was Daddy's erratic behavior, the ups and downs, the highs and lows, the "maybes" and the "go ask your moms!" that were most like the rolling swells of the blue sea. It was the loud radio playing whenever he was in the bathroom, the constant half-finished crossword puzzles in the magazine rack, the never-ending game of solitaire on the coffee table, and the clank, clank, jingle of the ice cubes in his cocktail glass that were most like the sea's fickle currents and deadly undertows. And in the end it was his unflappable command of the English language, his unshakable love affair with Bisquick and Spam, and his undeniable talent for knowing exactly when his boys were making fun of him behind his back that were most like the inevitable, swift pounding of the sea's angry surf.

Of course, I knew all this by now. I knew Daddy all too well. He was a familiar nemesis and I had conceded to the fact that my life would be spent battling his ego and struggling to push off his overpowering will, but like a fine stew laced heavily with bay leaves, I discovered that there were other archenemies in my life. There were other villains to battle, and it was the sea, of all things, that was the next obstacle in my path. The sea and Daddy! How much can one kid take? The sea shows no mercy; and it was on our transatlantic voyage that I experienced firsthand the sea's erratic and often "childish" behavior. It was an adventure I will not soon forget.

The prospect of portraying veteran horror film actor Bela Lugosi in a one-man show for twelve long months had lifted Daddy's spirits to new heights, and in preparation for our long trip he went on a spending spree that left most of the local merchants stripped bare of all their inventory, and MasterCard and Visa with permanent ear-to-ear smiles. He limoed from one posh establishment to the next, signing for literally thousands of dollars in clothing and various sundry items that he was certain we would need for our journey. It was the old Daddy, back in perfect form. It was the Bob Elliott the Manhattan gossip columns had so missed during his long Gold-Toe sock period, and in a way it was like the Michael Jackson Victory tour: Here was Bob Elliott, the fallen angel of Manhattan royalty, back to reclaim his ornate throne.

He got a nose job, an eye job, a tummy tuck, and his legs waxed. He had his ears cropped, his arches raised, and permanent shoulder pads implanted. He dyed his hair black, removed his wisdom teeth (by himself without anesthetic), and held his hand directly over a burning candle for thirty minutes every night. He was preparing for the biggest comeback of his career, and everything had to be just so.

He bought backpacks, sleeping bags, and two of everything from the Lillian Vernon catalog. He purchased two bicycles: an English racer for himself, and a three-speed red Stingray with raised handlebars and banana seat for me. I was thrilled. I couldn't wait to try out some "Pop-O-Wheelies" on the war-torn back roads of the English countryside, and for a brief period there, I thought to myself, "Hey, Daddy ain't so bad, after all!" Still, even by the opulent standards of the day, I knew Daddy was going a little overboard in the travel-necessities department.

Because I would be leaving school for a year, Herbert demanded that I make up my classes abroad. So our Tahitian cook, Mahala, was engaged to accompany us as combination manservant and tutor. I had always liked Mahala, and it comforted me to know

Daddy's Boy

he would be along. He was a tall, skinny dark man who spoke no English but possessed a wry, Bob Newhart-like sense of humor.

In the days before we left, Mahala found himself packing an odd assortment of "travel necessities" to say the least; Ouija boards, fondue sets, hundreds of boxes of paper clips, and a two-man submarine from Hammacher Schlemmer, complete with forty-amp thrusters and an air-supply system capable of maintaining up to one hundred cubic feet of oxygen. It was Daddy's fear of the high seas that prompted him to acquire the submarine, and I suppose having it along offered him some sort of security (false or not).

I woke the morning of our departure filled with uneasy anticipation. Maybe the trip was not a good idea, after all. What if we met with some horrible disaster at sea? What if we were shipwrecked? What if England was filled with queers? I ran to Daddy's room to express my misgivings, but Mommy said he had gone to D'Agostino's to pick up one last-minute "travel necessity." I felt cold fear coursing through my veins. Something dreadful was waiting for us out at sea, I just knew it. Daddy returned from D'Agostino's with three cases of Marshmallow Fluff, a horrible mixture of marshmallows and lard, usually spread on peanut-butter sandwiches. "I'm gonna make Fluffer-nutters and feed 'em to the li'l fishies when they swim up to the boat!" Daddy announced, and Mahala gave the universal sign for "This guy is crazy!" There was no time to talk with Daddy, no time to discuss the foreshadowing of doom I so clearly saw. No time to turn back.

The "boat" that Daddy planned to feed fish Fluffer-nutters from was the luxury liner *Andrea Doria*, and

Our Trip on the Andrea Doria

on December 28, 1970 I bid farewell to Mommy and my nine brothers and climbed the gangplank, fighting the onslaught of reporters and fans to board the ship. Onshore, Daddy offered some final departing words recorded forever by the grainy black-and-white newsreel footage of the day: "I'm looking forward to our trip. I'm sure it will be lots of fun . . . and let's just pray I don't throw up!" A cheer rose from the mass of well-wishers, and excitement rocked the dock as Daddy, too, boarded the ship. We stood on the forward deck, and as we waved good-bye through a mist of confetti and multicolored streamers, the magnificent *Andrea Doria* slid silently from its berth, steamed past Lady Liberty, and pressed on . . . out into the open ocean and the horror that lurked somewhere on the horizon.

Our first two days at sea passed smoothly. The waters were calm and glassy, and I spent much of my time exploring the ship, being tutored by Mahala, or playing shuffleboard with the older passengers, who seemed to populate the ship by a large majority. I liked being around the old folks; somehow they all reminded me of Uncle Sid and of what he had said: "Fame can be yours, too, my son!" I saw very little of Daddy in those first two days. He was cloistered away in our luxurious ten-cabin suite, studying his lines and working on his Bela Lugosi accent.

The *Andrea Doria*, in spite of all the media hype, exceeded my expectations tenfold. She was a grandiose vessel from bow to stern, and she was filled with so many wonderful and lavish sights that I couldn't help but stand in awe. There were mammoth marble staircases; elegant, turn-of-the-century chandeliers; intricately sculpted cherubs adorning every wall; baseboard heat and central air-conditioning throughout. There were barbershops, swimming pools, and a hockey rink. There was a rapid-transit monorail system to move passengers from one end of the boat to the other; and for those who just wanted to get away from it all, camping and hunting was permitted on the thirty-acre wildlife preserve located on B deck. Like the Hut, the *Andrea Doria* was a fairy-tale world.

The cuisine was simply divine. It was a combination of elegant, exotic offerings; flavors fit for kings, mixed in with the everyday foods of the common man and the blue-collar palate. The Donald Duck Special was my favorite: Salisbury steak cooked to perfection, beluga caviar chilled just so, and Laughing Cow cheese that was so smooth and creamy, it literally ran off your plate.

At night Mahala would take me to the Promenade Room where we would enjoy the evening's entertainment. The headliners were very good. They were a group of hippies who were on their way to a jazz concert in Devonshire and had traded entertainment for a free trip on the *Andrea Doria*. The band's lead singer was a tall, leggy blonde who wore hot pants and wedgie sandals. She had a wonderful quality to her voice not unlike Maureen McGovern's, and she sang songs of love and of hope. The ten-year-old son of Bob Elliott experienced for the first time a heart-mashing crush. The warm-up act, however, was an improvisational troupe called Laughs at Sea, and they really stank. No matter what "suggestions" they got from the audience, their improvs somehow always ended up in the Land of Oz. Still, the leggy blonde made the evenings in the Promenade Room more than worthwhile.

My crush on the songbird grew to obsession, so much so that I began to send flowers to her cabin, along with little notes: "I'll be in the audience tonight watching you. Think of me. Love and kisses, C. E." I guess the flowers, the notes, and the anonymous gifts I left outside her cabin door had alarmed her greatly, and she notified the ship's security. Eventually they found out that I was the secret admirer, and I got a stern talking-to by the purser: "If you don't stop bugging that lady, we're gonna throw you into the brig, you little rich brat!" I tried to explain that it had all been a simple misunderstanding and that that would be the end of it.

Ironically, only Mahala could understand my emotions at the time. We strolled about the many decks, and I found him to be a good listener with a compassionate ear; although I could not understand a word he said, I grew even more appreciative of his dry, Robert Benchley-esque wit.

I was experiencing first love, puppy love, an adolescent crush—but at the time it felt like so much more. I remember going to Daddy for some heart-to-heart father-son advice. But, alas, we just ended up arguing as usual. The argument had nothing to do with my infatuation for the singer; instead, it had to do with Daddy's Bela Lugosi impersonation—I noticed that Daddy had been walking around with a limp, and on the rare occasions when he ventured topside, he used a cane. When I asked him what had happened, he seemed annoyed, saying, "Nothing, go mind your own business." When I insisted on knowing how he hurt his leg, he just blew up. "Listen, Bela Lugosi's right leg was shorter than his left leg! I'm trying to experience what it would be like to go through life like that, okay? Now why don't you get out of my hair and go play shuffleboard with the old farts!"

He had never yelled at me like that before. I felt hurt and angry. I thought to myself, "I'd like to tell the 'old farts' what the great Bob Elliott is really like!" There I was in the uncharted waters of romance, desperately seeking advice from an experienced hand in those matters, and instead we get into a fight about Bela Lugosi's leg lengths. "I hate you! I hate you!" I announced, and I ran back to B deck to calm myself by a peaceful, babbling brook.

I wasn't sure what I wanted to do. Perhaps run away. Steal Daddy's two-man submarine, slip overboard in the dead of night, and get away . . . head south, 'round Cape Horn, and make land somewhere in Mahala's Tahiti, or perhaps the Fiji Islands. But would a hundred cubic feet of oxygen be enough for such a voyage? Oh, it was a crazy plan, one that would be doomed from the start.

I decided not to do anything, nothing at all. That's how I would get back at Daddy. My revenge would be a silent and simple one: I would just not tell Daddy that Lugosi's legs were the same length. "Let him go onstage with a limp!" I thought to myself. He'll be the laughingstock of the entire British theatrical community. He'll never be able to look Andrew Lloyd Webber in the face again!

On December 31, we woke to a violent storm at sea. The ship pitched and yawed so drastically that we were all thrown from our bunks. Fine china came crashing out of our kitchenette cabinets, and Mahala's prized collection of political campaign buttons went flying every which way.

"What the hell is going on?" demanded Daddy.

"It's a storm!" I shouted back.

"Impossible! These are first-class cabins!"

Of course, it *was* possible. Rich or poor, arrived or unarrived, royalty or not, on December 31, the *Andrea Doria* rocked in all classes. As the angry tempest raged throughout the day and into the evening, my vision of death and destruction seemed imminent. The ship was taking a beating. It was the sea versus the *Andrea Doria*, and I think all aboard wondered how the fine lady would fair in such a battle. I know, inside, the storm terrified me.

In spite of everything, the ship's daily routine remained unchanged. It was New Year's Eve, and everyone prepared to send off the old and ring in the new in high style. There would be a giant celebration in the Promenade Room, and all were invited. Being the only superstar aboard, Daddy received a special invitation to dine at the captain's table, and I remember thinking what an honor that was.

We dressed to the teeth in our identical white sequined tuxedos and adorned our heads with powdered barrister wigs (as was the fashion of the elitist rich at the time). We boarded the monorail and sped off to the Promenade Room, leaving Mahala in front of the TV, oblivious of the mad storm outside and completely engrossed in an episode of *Petticoat Junction*.

The Promenade Room was jammed to capacity

that fateful night, and as we made our entrance, Laughs at Sea were just finishing up their last improv . . . something about Dorothy and the Scarecrow riding off together in a forklift. The room stood on its feet and gave Daddy and me a standing ovation. "They love our outfits!" Daddy whispered, and we were ushered to the captain's table.

A balding, portly fellow with an amusing lisp, the captain was quite different from what I had expected. "It-th an honor to have you with uth, Mithter Elliott," he said, and then he introduced us to the other people at the table.

As the captain rounded the table with introductions I noticed that Daddy was giggling uncontrollably at the poor man's speech impediment, and I thought to myself, "My father is a child." I could hardly pay attention, and I can only vaguely remember our fellow diners; I know there was Mr. and Mrs. Rosen, on their way to visit their two-year-old grandson; Mr. Martin, a middle-aged bachelor and haberdasher by trade: Mr. Rogo, a beefy ex-detective, and his new bride, Linda (a beefy ex-prostitute); and the Reverend Scott, whom I pegged right away as one of those "do-gooder" types—the kind of guy who likes to get involved in everyone's problems.

"I wath jutht ekthplaining to everyone how common thith type of thtorm ith in theeth wateth," said the captain, and Daddy, straining against laughing out loud in the man's face, retorted with, "Really?" and his laugh exited his nose, forcing a sneeze. The captain looked perplexed, but his attention was suddenly drawn to the blinking red light on his private telephone. "Hello?" He paused, very concerned. "I'll be right there." He hung up and excused himself, and Daddy let out the hysterics he'd been trying so hard to hold in.

I think we all felt that the captain's sudden departure signaled "danger ahead," but still, we all managed a little small talk, all except Daddy, who was still giggling inanely. The discussion was diverse. We were all interested in the many different vitamins that Mr. Martin kept popping. Detective Rogo told a cute and amusing story about the first time he and his prostitute wife met, and the Reverend Scott pushed his progressive interpretation of faith. I became lost in a gaze across the room at the giant floor-to-celing Christmas tree—mesmerized by the shimmering icicles that hung from it.

Onstage, Laughs at Sea was now replaced by the headliners, and for me everything else in the room stopped. The leggy blonde came onstage singing her songs of love and hope. They seemed especially apropos, considering the mad storm outside.

"There's got to be a morning after . . ." she sang, "If we can make it to the shore; Oh, can't you see the morning after, it's waiting right outside the door."

I felt as if she were singing just to me. I knew that if we made it through the storm, I would have to make her notice me somehow, and I decided that I would have to do something very drastic.

"A toast!" exclaimed the Reverend Scott.

"What to?" someone asked.

"To love!" he said thoughtfully.

"Hear! Hear!" cheered the ex-prostitute, and we all clinked our champagne glasses. ("Yes, to love," I thought to myself, "to love and to that leggy blonde. She's never gonna forget me!")

Up on the bridge, hell was about to break loose. The lookout had spotted a giant tidal wave off the starboard side, headed directly toward the *Andrea Doria*. "Oh, my God!" was the helpless cry of the captain as the giant wall of water came bearing down upon us.

In the Promenade Room, everyone again stood, this time counting down the final seconds of 1970. In my head were nothing but dark thoughts as I stared strangely at the blond singer. "You're gonna know my name, lady! Just wait and see, you're gonna beg to be my girlfriend." I had really snapped.

"Five, four, three, two, one . . . Happy New Year!"

We all hugged and kissed, and even Daddy and I exchanged a warm handshake. It was a good moment, and a good new year full of hope . . . but I was possessed. I began to weave my way through the crowd, headed for the singer in the wedgie sandals. Everything seemed like it was in slow motion to me. I'm not sure what I was going to do when I reached her. Was I going to wish her a Happy New Year? Or was I going to do something else, something bad? . . . but suddenly it happened . . . the monster wave hit the *Andrea Doria* broadside, and we all felt the numbing thud.

Yelps of joy for the new year cross-faded into horrified screams as the ballroom began to do the unthinkable. It began to turn upside down.

I tumbled to the farthest wall. All around me chairs, silverware, candles, and toupees came crashing down. A man to my left shouted, "Wow, does that

CHRIS ELLIOTT'S
PERSONAL COLLECTION OF PHOTOS

Daddy and Daddy's boy—in happier times.

Fox Run, or the "Hut" (circa 1970).

One of my glamorous birthday parties. It was sheer hell!

Here we are in our matching sailor outfits
and Bella Abzug floppy hats.

After Daddy lost his hair I had to wear
this stupid latex bald wig.

Topside with some fans, during our
doomed voyage on the *Andrea Doria*.

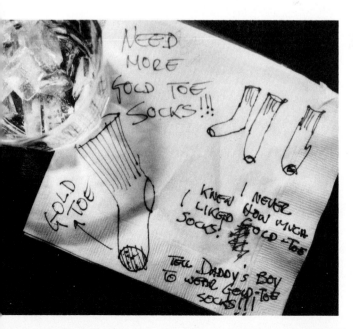

Some of Daddy's
insane doodles
during his
Gold-Toe sock
period.

Snapshot of Elvis that I took in the fall of '86
(from *My Search for Elvis* by Chris Elliott).

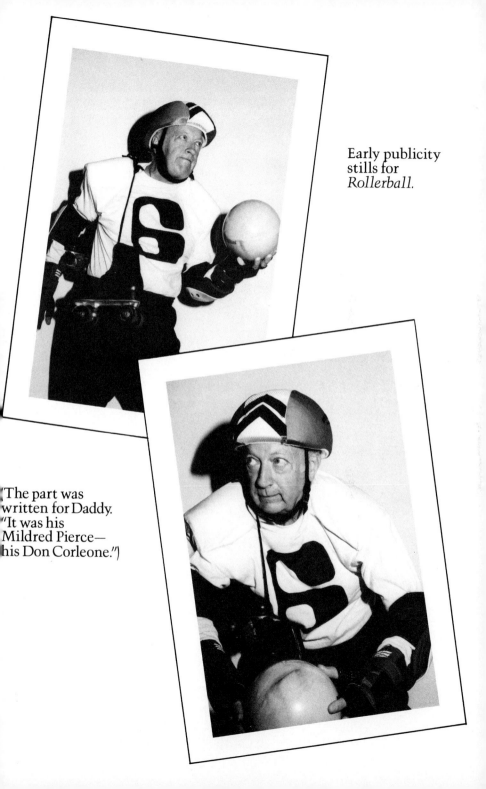

Early publicity
stills for
Rollerball.

("The part was
written for Daddy.
"It was his
Mildred Pierce—
his Don Corleone.")

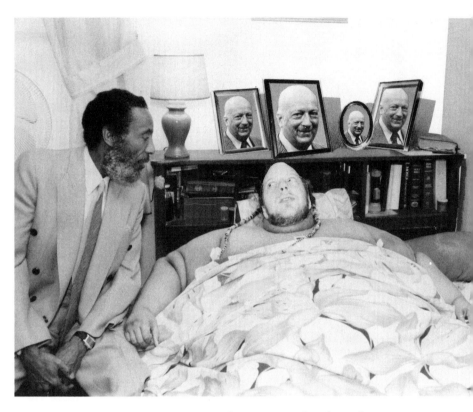

Here I am in my fat teens, with a friend.

I emerge from my shell of blubber
an absolute Adonis!

Risking it all on the high wire between Bob's Big Towers.
It was my final cry to be noticed!

BOB ELLIOTT'S
PERSONAL COLLECTION OF PHOTOS
(Taken by Harley Freeney last summer)

Here I am enjoying my vacation in Maine
(before I found out that I had to work on this book).

Reading Chris's prologue.

This is the gag shot that Harley took of me at the town dump.

The
Cape Hatteras
lighthouse.

Working on my PXG-297 game.

The Kittery toll on I-95.

Trying to get chapter eight away from Moxie.

Finnan haddie.

hurt!" as the giant grand piano slammed into him, pinning him to the wall. The intricately sculpted cherubs flew about like demon angels from hell. It was complete chaos. I glanced up and saw that the huge Christmas tree was hanging completely inverted. The *Andrea Doria* had capsized but miraculously was still afloat. Above, the banquet tables were still attached to the ballroom floor, which was now the ceiling. A man dangled precariously from one of the tables, and I watched in horror as he let loose his hold, falling about a hundred feet and smashing down into one of the giant chandeliers resting on the floor.

I couldn't watch anymore. I closed my eyes and tried to wish it all away. I didn't know if I was dead or alive. After a moment the horrible sounds of twisting metal and cracking bones were replaced by stunned silence. I wondered if the leggy blond singer had made it . . . and then I don't remember anything else.

When next I opened my eyes, I was waist-deep in icy water and entombed in the two-man submarine from Hammacher Schlemmer. "Prepare to dive!" The command was Daddy's, and I looked to my left but everything was a blur. Daddy's powdered wig was matted to his head, and he was trying to figure out the controls of the sub. "Dive! Dive! Dive!" he hollered, and then I blacked out again.

When my wrinkled lids unveiled my piercing blue eyes once more, I saw that we were indeed submerged in the cold, dark Atlantic, and I began to shake. "Here, you better eat something," said Daddy, and he handed me a jar of Marshmallow Fluff.

"What happened?" I asked.

"You must have hit your head. You've been out for a week."

"Where are we?"

"Oh, about twenty or so miles off the New England coast, crusing southwest at about five knots . . . we're going home, son."

"Home?" I was still dazed.

"Yeah, after that *Andrea Doria* thing I figured to hell with the one-man show. They can get Howard Cosell. He's better for the part than me, anyway. I think what we need is a little R and R back at the Hut."

Everything he was saying, I understood; and yet it all seemed so unreal to me. We were actually puttering along the ocean's bottom, eating Marshmallow Fluff in a submarine from Hammacher Schlemmer. I looked at Daddy, and his wig had dried in an odd, askew fashion; he now looked like Professor Irwin Corey.

Along the way Daddy filled me in on what had happened, although he didn't go into details, perhaps to spare me from the absolute horror of it all. He told me that the ship was hit by a tidal wave and had capsized. He said that Reverend Scott had gathered everyone together at the captain's table and convinced them that the only way to survive would be to climb up through the wreckage of the ship, into the propeller shaft, and out of the bottom hull. He told me that he had been one of those who felt that the reverend's plan was ludicrous and had chosen to stay behind. But as soon as the Promenade Room had filled with cold water, he realized he had made an error in judgment. Then he said that Mahala, the good servant, appeared like a guardian angel with the two-man submarine and a month's supply of Marshmallow Fluff.

To this day I don't know what exactly became of Mahala. Daddy was very vague on what happened next.

"Where's Mahala?" I asked.

"Who? Oh, ah, well, Mahala couldn't make it," Daddy said, obviously hiding something.

It didn't occur to me then, but it is clear to me now that Daddy simply ordered Mahala to stay behind. There was room for only two in the submarine, although if he had not brought along so many jars of Marshmallow Fluff we could have fit another person in. But Mahala, being the loyal servant, obeyed and stayed with the ship. I am not saying that Daddy actually killed Mahala (lawyers, please take note), I am simply stating that perhaps he was in some way responsible for his death. At any rate, Mahala was gone. He had saved our lives, but I would never see him again; and still, today, I miss his Jack Benny-esque sense of humor.

Our voyage underwater lasted another week . . . another horrible week. Looking back, it probably would have been the ideal opportunity for Daddy and me to get to know each other all over again, to heal the wounds that had severed us, to regain a normal father-and-son relationship, but we didn't even try. Instead we passed the time playing geography, singing show tunes, and cracking each other's knuckles.

We took turns navigating and keeping watch. We

surfaced once or twice to see if we could spot land, but no such luck. Days meshed together and hours lingered like the last guest at a cocktail party. Hunger set in. Hunger for real food: No more Fluffernutters—I wanted the Donald Duck Special. I began to get light-headed. I began to hallucinate. I was sure that Tony Orlando was swimming alongside the submarine out in the murky water.

The third time we surfaced, we found, to our surprise, that our crude navigational skills had paid off, after all. We were in the mouth of New York Harbor, not thirty feet from Battery Park.

A huge crowd of spectators were gathered on the shore. We could hear them cheering, "Hip, hip, hooray!" I had never been so happy to see Daddy's fans as I was that day, and I looked at Daddy in a different light.

"How wonderful to have such loyal fans," I mused.

"Aye . . . most of them are jerks!" he said, and I realized that no matter in what light I looked at Daddy, he would always be the same.

We began to cruise over to the dock, and as we approached, I noticed a large banner held high amid the crowd. The banner read, WELCOME BACK, TONY! and I also observed that everyone was wearing yellow ribbons around their arms or on their lapels. I grabbed a pair of binoculars from the emergency kit and focused in just in time to catch Tony Orlando swimming up to the dock and exiting the water wearing a skintight Speedo bikini. The crowd went nuts. They hoisted him up and carried him away, cheering. "Hip, hip, hooray!" These were not Daddy's fans. There were only a couple of winos left onshore when we climbed onto the dock in our drenched tuxedos and matted wigs.

"I wonder where everyone went?" Daddy pondered, and as we hailed a cab I felt in my pocket and pulled out the shot glass Uncle Sid had given me as a lucky charm. I've never gone anywhere without it since.

We would find out later that Tony Orlando had just finished a three-lap swim around Manhattan Island at the very moment that we surfaced in Battery Park, and I had not hallucinated at all.

And so my forecast of doom on the morning of our departure had come true. The sea had gone crazy on us. I returned to my studies at Herbert, and Daddy returned to his career. The disaster left its telltale signs on both our personalities and affected us differently. I began to gain weight, a lot of weight . . . and Daddy could never shake his annoying, uncontrollable giggle.

Life proceeded, but the next six years would be even more horrible and even more shocking than the previous eleven, and I would have to make a choice between remaining Daddy's Boy or becoming my own man.

I often relive the tragedy of the *Andrea Doria* in my nightmares, but more often than not, the image most embedded in my soul is that of the leggy blond singer in wedgie sandals. My obsession was a sickness that had lit a dangerous fuse in my mind. I have long since gotten over her, but I still occasionally wonder "What if?" What if the ship had not capsized? What would I have done? The leggy blonde never made it off the doomed *Andrea Doria*, and in a way she was the luckiest of us all. If that tidal wave had not hit just when it did, there's really no telling what I could have done. (I was really insane those couple of days at sea.)

"There's got to be a morning after . . ." she sang. Thank God, for her sake, there wasn't one.

6/ Rebuttal to Chapter Five

THIS MIGHT BE AS GOOD A SPOT AS any for me to fess up and admit I think this whole thing is a hoax. All these pages of highly charged drama my son is churning out are make-believe, right? And the ideas stolen, to boot.

After all, I certainly recognize *The Poseidon Adventure* when I see it, as I'm sure you do.

July and August saw a record heat wave in Maine and most of the country, and an overabundance of hot air generated by the presidential campaigns. The combination was more than enough to make one sick at the mere mention of finnan haddie, so I shelved my project in favor of cooler pursuits. Like buying a new car for the first time in a decade.

I hadn't really given last rites to the '59 Galaxie, but the odds against it getting us where we wanted to go were growing. Complicating things was the fact that I talked myself into buying it in the State of Maine in the month of July.

With the checkbook in my back pocket, but determined to be my own master in the proverbial car salesman/customer charade, I stepped onto the dealer's property one morning.

After a good three minutes of uninterrupted private browsing, an adder-eyed salesman pounced, just as I'd heard they did.

He began pointing out some of the features of the vehicles: their four wheels, telescoping antennas, tinted glass, and other items I probably would have overlooked.

He explained rack-and-pinion steering to me, and I helped him along with questions like, "I suppose my mileage may vary—depending on my own driving habits?"

The result of this foray on the automobile world was as predictable as when Ollie, on a camping trip, tells Stan to "go out into the woods and bring back a bunch of faggots." I bought a car.

In this one reckless action I had burdened myself with an end-of-the-model-year vehicle, all the details of insurance and maintenance that Avis used to take care of, plus an annual mid-July drive to the Big Apple to register the thing.

About the only redeeming feature of the whole business was the little game I developed, based on my new license plate, which happened to be PXG-297. If you're ever in New York State driving— or afoot—you'll find it fun to play, and I think you'll be as impressed as I was, by the frequency with which you'll spot one of the letters or numbers.

Following are the Official Rules.

Rebuttal to Chapter Five

THE PXG-297 GAME

Object

To find one or more of the letters *P, X,* or *G,* and the numbers 2, 9, or 7, in other New York State license plates, and shouting your discovery to your opponent.

Notes

1. Only New York State plates count.
2. Only plates with letter groupings first, followed by numbers. (Do not use plates with numbers first, followed by letters!)
3. Letter and number groups may be in any order.
4. Taxis and commercial vehicles are excluded.

Challenge

To outpoint your opponent before he or she gets the "hang" of the game.

Scoring

TOP SCORE: A plate with all characters (P, X, and G and 297) in any order.

> *Example:* XPG-927 or GPX-279
> (20 Points)
> *You shout:* "XPG-927!" or
> "GPX-279!"

2ND BEST: A plate with P, X, and G in *proper* order, followed by 2, 9, and 7 in any order.

> *Example:* PXG-927 or PXG-279
> (17 Points)
> *You shout:* "PXG-927!" or
> "PXG-279!"

3RD BEST: A plate with P, X, and G in *any* order, followed by 2, 9, and 7 in proper order.

> *Example:* XPG-297 or GPX-297
> (16 Points)
> *You shout:* "XPG-297!" or
> "GPX-297!"

4TH BEST: Any two of the PXG letters and any two of the 297 numbers.

> *Example:* XPL-294 or PGR-924 (15 Points)
> *You shout:* "XP-29!" or "PG-92!"

5TH BEST: One letter and one number:

> *Example:* PTN-961 or XDE-869 (12 Points)
> *You shout:* "P-9!" or "X-9!"

6TH BEST: One letter *or* one number (most frequently found).

> *Example:* "XBD-384" or
> "DLR-265" (10 Points)
> *You shout:* "X!" or "2!"

Rebuttal to Chapter Five

ADVANCED (OR DOUBLED) PXG-297

1. Spot plates with doubled letters or numbers.

> *Example:* PPF-299 or AXX-737 (49 Points)
> *You shout:* "PP-99!" or "XX-77!"

2. Spot plates with one letter or one number away from PXG-297.

> *Example:* PX*H*-297 or PXG-29*8* (30 Points)
> *You shout:* "PX-297!" or "PXG-29!"

3. Game limited to winning plates seen within a pre-agreed number of miles (if you are motoring).
4. Parked cars don't count.

Note

As you practice the game you will find your skill at spotting letter and number combinations and shouting them to your opponent will improve until, on a short drive or walk, you can easily score 130–165 points before your initial enthusiasm falters.

Game may be played while driving alone, in which case shouting is not necessary. (Nor is it recommended.)

7 / The Thumb-wrestle Miracle

I'M SORRY. I APOLOGIZE IN ADVANCE. I am fully aware that I was forbidden to read any of my dad's rebuttals prior to this book's first printing, nor was I, under any circumstance, to refer to or comment on his rebuttals in my chapters, but I'm afraid I'm just going to have to bend the rules.

I have just come from my publisher's office, and while His Majesty was down the hall screaming at one of his underlings, I took notice of a file on his desk marked "Bob Elliott's Rebuttals," and I must admit I could not resist a peek. Frankly, Dear Reader, I must tell you that I am not in the least bit amused by the pure propaganda, the litany of lies, and the sheer nonsense that my dad is filling up his pages with and polluting *my* book with. Who in heck-tarnation does he think he is?

He's been up there in Maine, in his summer cottage, walking around in his boxer shorts, eating lobster, doing crossword puzzles, and obviously getting sunstroke. I mean, what is his problem? It's like something out of *The Shining*. He's been isolated up there too long. The remoteness of the place has gotten to him. I think he's gone a little nutty. He's soft as a melon!

I never, in my life, owned any Jenny Lind records. I don't have the slightest idea who Jenny Lind is anyway! What is it with this dumb finnan haddie contest, and who cares? Someone had to tell me that finnan haddie was fish; I thought maybe it was an old vaudeville comedy act. ". . . the heron gulls, gray and grizzled . . ." Give me a break!

Maybe they have the red tide up there in Maine this summer. That must be it: The lobsters are being tainted by the red-tide poison, and Daddy is eating the lobsters and the poison is turning his brain into corned-beef hash.

What was that lighthouse thing all about? And that stupid, stupid PXG-007 game, or whatever the hell the numbers are! The man knows that game drives me nuts. Why on earth would he subject my readers to it? I strongly suspect the guy is not even reading my chapters. He hardly comments on *anything* relating to my chapters. Could it possibly be that he is not reading them? What an arrogant display of bumptiousness on his part.

Now, I care about this book: I want it to be good. I admit I may have exaggerated a few details here and there, but it's only to enhance an otherwise dull story. No, that's not what I mean. The exaggerations are simply to add spice to a lukewarm stew. At any rate, the story has to be told . . . and it will be. Why won't Daddy just play along?

It just goes to show what I've had to put up with

all my life. His reluctance to use his allotted pages as a forum for serious answers to my chapters is conclusive proof that the man likes to bug me, and so, without even realizing it, he is irrefutably supporting all my inculpations. Sorry, Dad, you lose. You're trying in your own subtle way to throw a wrench into the works . . . to draw attention away from the true facts . . . well, your little plan just backfired. I don't care, go ahead and write about your Finnan Haddie Festival. I'm going to continue, undaunted, to tell the true, horrifying story. The truth will set you free, Daddy. When all is finished, the world will not be interested in your little fish festival, for they will know the ultimate, shocking truth of my upbringing! And so, dear Daddy, if you are reading this now, brace yourself, for I am about to tell all; and for crying out loud, get off the shellfish . . . it's screwing with your marbles!

I followed the footprints as best I could. Occasionally they would disappear and I would have to rely on instinct, and my best guess, as to which direction he would take. I followed his trail deep into the gloomy woods. Nightfall came, then dawn, then nightfall again, then dawn again. It was the tenth day, and I estimated that I had walked at least twenty miles into the Adirondacks.

On the eleventh day I discovered a clump of shaggy hair clinging to a bayberry branch in a bog, not far from my campsite. Upon close inspection I determined that the hair was gray, although it still showed traces of black dye. He was close. He was very close . . . and then I heard it; a kind of huffing and puffing, and then a growling sound and a gnaw-

ing sound, like some kind of wild animal. The noises
were coming from behind me. Slowly I unsnapped
my holster and pulled out my revolver. I was scared.
I summoned all my guts and turned around. My
heart stopped; there he was, not ten feet away, wearing what was left of his famous sequinned jumpsuit.
He was . . .

I'm sorry, Dear Reader, but I think I picked up the
wrong notes. The above passage belongs to my book
entitled *My Search for Elvis*, in which I prove beyond
a shadow of a doubt that the King is still alive. Here
now is Chapter Seven of *Daddy's Boy*, entitled "The
Thumb-wrestle Miracle." I hope you enjoy it, and I
apologize for the mix-up.

It was now the mid-1970s and I was to all intents
and purposes an undeniable blimp. I was huge. Adolescence had unleashed an insatiable appetite that
raged inside me day in and day out. I just could not
stop eating, and family and friends pondered the
curious transformation of cute kid into monstrous
freak. What was happening to me? What was going
wrong?

I could come up with plenty of excuses, but I know
there was only one real cause: Daddy. There were
some obvious lingering, emotional scars from our
disaster on the *Andrea Doria*, but my new compulsion with eating was a direct result of fifteen years of
total domination . . . fifteen years on a tight leash
. . . having to act and appear precisely as Daddy
prescribed. Getting fat was the only way I knew to
disobey Daddy. It was the only tool at hand that I
could use to crush the mold that I was being forced

to fit into. Getting fat enabled me to develop my own personality, to be my own man, to form my own image . . . even if that image was starting to look an awful lot like Fatty Arbuckle.

Oddly enough, Daddy did not seem unsympathetic to the plague of obesity I was afflicted with. He only referred to me as Barrel Bottom and Blubber Butt when we were in public, refraining from using nicknames around the house, and I thought that was kind of him. He posted WARNING: FAT BOY LIVES HERE signs outside the Hut, so that little children wouldn't be frightened if they caught sight of me when they walked by, and I thought that was considerate of him. He opened a McDonald's in the north wing of the Hut, and he presented me with a huge stack of coupons that allowed me to eat there for free, and I thought that was pretty darn nice of the guy. All in all, he seemed to go out of his way to try to make life slightly easier for me around the house. He still wanted me to dress like him, but now all my clothes were manufactured by Goodyear. It seemed Daddy just didn't want to admit that I had a problem.

"He's just a growing boy," he would say. "There's nothing wrong with putting a little meat on his bones!" It was the understatement of the decade.

For breakfast I usually ate three to four pounds of bacon, two dozen eggs, six loaves of Wonder Bread, and at least fifty Pop-Tarts. The remainder of the day's consumption would escalate frighteningly from there. I was putting more than just a little meat on my bones. By the time I was sixteen years old, I had ballooned to an alarming eight hundred and fifty-five pounds, and Daddy was not only forced to hire a crane to carry me to and from school but also he was now forced to admit that I had a real weight problem.

It was a wonderful era, and yet I was a miserable kid leading a miserable existence. After all, it was the mid-seventies and if only I could have stopped eating for a second, maybe I could have taken part in the excitement of my generation, a generation eager to come of age and grasp the reins of power. My classmates' faces were all etched with the anticipation of an electric, new era, but alas, my face remained etched with hunger and stained by blueberry pie.

This was the time in Manhattan when the streets were filled with the magical music that seemed to set afire the pulse of the great metropolis. The enchanting strains of Queen's "Bohemian Rhapsody," the compelling demands of the Starland Vocal Band's "Afternoon Delight," and the haunting echoes of Paper Lace's "The Night Chicago Died" all emanated from the old Philco. At Herbert, the high-school chorus performed a medley of Jethro Tull hits including "Cross-Eyed Mary" and "Locomotive Breath." I still can remember our conductor, Mr. Yohan, adding his own personal touch when he rehearsed us. "Okay, let's have sopranos only on 'snot is running down his nose . . .' and then altos and tenors strong on 'greasy fingers smearing shabby clothes,' okay? From the top!" It was a wonderful time, but I didn't think so back then. Back then all I cared about was where my next club sandwich was coming from.

Daddy's Boy

Daddy picked up on the popular new music craze and for a year or so concentrated his career entirely on recording. As he aged, his voice took on a raspy quality that enabled him to record tunes with a slightly Motown feeling. "Ol' Pink Eyes," as Daddy was now called (due to a chronic case of conjunctivitis), was back on top of the charts. "Ricky Don't Lose That Number" was his biggest hit. The album went platinum, and he sold out Madison Square Garden three nights in a row. As a whole new generation of fans discovered Bob Elliott, I wallowed in his shadow, eating constantly and sinking deeper and deeper into the quicksand of his career, which now engulfed me and choked my every breath.

"Fame can be yours, too, my son, ummmmm!" Old Uncle Sid's words had moved into a three-bedroom apartment in my brain and had left their illegible signature on a lifelong lease with my soul. Ironically I wanted fame now more than ever. All Uncle Sid could do was smile and say, "Someday, kid, maybe when you drop a few pounds."

I wanted to be a superstar. I wanted to be recognized on the street, to be chased by hordes of screaming teenage girls, to be imitated by Fred Travalena on *The Copy Cats*. I wanted to be interviewed on *60 Minutes*. I wanted to be a judge on *Dance Fever*, and I wanted them to film a made-for-TV movie about my life starring Shaun Cassidy as me. I wanted to be immortalized in the famous Manhattan Wax Museum, to have my own star on the Broadway Walk of Fame, and to put my paw prints in the wet concrete outside Szechuan Palace on Eighty-ninth and Columbus. I wanted to train the lions on

Circus of the Stars. I wanted my own line of polyester sport-coats, and I wanted to do commercials for Coca-Cola and Jell-O Pudding Pops. Most of all, I wanted to surpass Daddy; to be bigger and better than the great Bob Elliott.

Once at a family picnic in our backyard, I made a complete fool of myself by challenging Daddy to a father-and-son thumb wrestle. Ever since I was a little boy, thumb wrestling had been a big part of the "horsing-around" hour, and Daddy was an expert thumb wrestler. The object was to pin your opponent's thumb down with your own and hold it down for a count of five, but the trick was to do it with a certain amount of style. Daddy exhausted himself trying to drum into his sons proper thumb-wrestling techniques, but we were not quick learners, and not one of us could ever beat Daddy.

So here I was, the fat teenager, the eight hundred and fifty-five pound punk challenging the expert . . . challenging Bob Elliott, not just to a thumb wrestle but to a battle of wills . . . challenging him to measure up to his own image . . . taunting him to wage war against his own prodigy, his alter ego, the fat son he'd spent years shaping and forming.

"Come on, old man, let's see what you got!" I demanded, thrusting my thumb in his face. All around me my nine brothers each "gulped" out loud, and I heard Mommy say, "Oh, my." The family stood frozen in shocked dismay. As always, Daddy maintained his cool-as-a-cucumber composure and meticulously wiped the remnants of a deviled-ham sandwich from the corners of his mouth. "Do you know what you're saying, little man?"

"Oh, I know exactly what I'm saying, little big

man!" I retorted in my best Clint Eastwood. He took a moment to scan me up and down with his icy blue steel eyes. He sensed my nervousness and my fear, but for the first time in his life he admired my spunk. "Then so it shall be!" he announced.

Immediately a tangle of arms rushed in, sweeping the sandwiches and the potato salad off the picnic table. All the patio furniture was pushed aside, and amid the chaos of preparation for the match, Daddy and I remained still, locked eye to eye, shooting daggers into each other's windows.

"Don't let His Highness scare you," whispered Bob, Jr., Number Six as he massaged my shoulders. "You can do it. Whip his ass! Do it for all of us!" I looked around me and all nine towheads were giving me the thumbs-up. I felt as though I were about to take my first step into manhood.

Daddy removed his Western-style shirt, revealing a firm, hairy chest, the topography of which was crisscrossed with long scars, painful reminders of his fencing days, and decorated in colorful, absurd tattoos (embarrassing imprints from his circus years). When I removed my stretch shirt, boneless blubber rolled out in all directions. There was simply no comparing my giant, sluglike form to Daddy's Buster Crabbe physique.

"Let us begin!" Daddy commanded, and high atop the east balcony one of the servants blew a horn.

The Elliott Clan gathered in a semicircle around the picnic table. Daddy sat on one side, resting his elbows on the table, as if we were about to arm-wrestle. I sat opposite him in a big hammock seat, specially designed to accommodate my fat butt.

Mother blindfolded us, as was the proper procedure for professional thumb wrestling. Before I knew it, our hands were clasped tightly together and we were engaged in hand-to-hand, thumb-to-thumb combat.

My memory rewound to the instructions Daddy had tried to pound into us back when the "horsing-around" hour always followed the harp concerts, back in the good old days of the Elliott household. I listened closely to his voice echoing inside my head: "Always anticipate your opponent's every move! Never give your opponent an opening! Clean and clip your thumbnails adequately before each match! And, most importantly, remember to be quick! You're quick, quick, as quick as a firefly!"

Well, I knew I wasn't as quick as a firefly. I could hardly move my fat thumb a quarter of an inch without breaking out in a cold sweat.

The only thing I had going for me was my mind. Could I outwit my dad? Fat chance!

His nimble thumb knocked and poked at mine. Each knock and each poke produced a dull thudding noise, like a punch sound effect from a *Rocky* movie. One moment he would caress my thumb's thickest region, and in the next instant he would slam into the digit's midsection with battering-ram power. All this was legal. Daddy was winning; my exuberance and youthful vigor were no match for his years of experience and his Boston cunning.

He nudged away at my thumb, swaying it to the left, then to the right, pushing and squeezing it, playing with it like it was a child's squeaky toy. I was straining what was left of every single muscle in my body, and I struggled beneath the blindfold not to show my anguish. I could feel my face turning red-hot as blood from broken vessels rushed to the skin's surface. I was sure all would be lost soon.

The battle raged for an eternity. Occasionally Daddy would allow me to land a blow, at which time I could tell that the sheer weight of my thumb had buckled his; but then, like lightning, he would come back with a combination nudge, knock, poke, and squeeze that would send my obese digit reeling. There would be no mercy. He was going to come in for the kill.

Then something happened—I'm still not sure what it was. It was a miracle of sorts. I remember rolling my thumb around, preparing to send it down in defeat. It must have caught Daddy broadside, because as my thumb made its descent, it took his with it. Before I knew it, I heard a crunching sound as Daddy's knuckles cracked and his poor thumb was squashed, trapped beneath my huge freak thumb.

I could hear my mother counting out loud as Daddy's hand thrashed wildly to and fro in an attempt to loosen his thumb. "One, two, three, four . . . five! Winner!"

Oh, my God, I'd done it. I'd won! I couldn't believe it. I had challenged the old man to wage war and I'd been victorious. I was free. I was my own man. The heavy iron door to the dungeon opened up and I took my first breath of fresh, untainted air. "Welcome to manhood, Chris!" I thought to myself. "It's been a long, hard road, but you're here now and you're going to make it. You showed the old man. You whipped his butt for yourself, and for your nine brothers to boot!"

All around me I could hear the whoops and cheers of my family, and I pulled off my blindfold, shouting to the highest turrets of the Hut, "I did it! I did it! I won! Yeah! Yeah! Yeah!"

Miracles can still happen in this world, but we must know to grasp them quickly and bask in their results fully, for they are fleeting. A miracle can only survive if it is allowed to survive. (Thank you, thank you very much.)

For a second everything was a blur, until the image in front of me fused together. It was an image I was not prepared for, and it shocked me. There was my daddy with an ear-to-ear grin pasted on his face, and I thought that was an odd countenance for someone who had just lost a thumb wrestle. Then I perceived why he was smiling: The Elliott Clan was gathered all around him, hugging, caressing, and congratulating him. Mommy gave him a big kiss and said, "Great job, honey, you really creamed him!" and Bob, Jr., Number Six lifted Daddy's hand high in the air and proclaimed, "Bob Elliott, the winner!"

I'd been had. My miracle had been snatched out from underneath me. My own mother and my own brothers had betrayed me. They had all seen me win, but not one of them had the nerve to call Daddy a loser. My hands were tied. There was nothing I could do but go ahead and congratulate Daddy myself.

"You see, Chris, I'm older and stronger than you," Daddy said with a nasty twinkle in his pink eyes. "I'll always win!" And then he threw his head back and let out an unearthly, maniacal cackle.

The thumb fight thrust me deeper yet into a world of black darkness. The joy, the fun, the frolic that should surround a child was just not there, and I remained locked in a personal isolation tank, alone with my fears and tortured by insecurities.

I had to keep reminding myself that a miracle had in fact occurred. I had beaten Daddy at his own game. If there was any solace to be had, it was that in his heart Daddy knew I'd won, too, and he was going to have to live with that fact.

My grades plummeted drastically. The only things I excelled at were gaining weight and acne. Each day after school when the giant crane dropped me home, I would retreat into the basement of the Hut and play in my fantasy, talk-show world, bantering witty jabs back and forth with a life-size cardboard cutout of Johnny Carson. Upstairs, Daddy diligently prepared for the starring role in the upcoming movie *Rollerball*, a futuristic adventure about a deadly sport played on roller skates. The part had been written for Daddy. It was the role of a lifetime, his Don Corleone, his Mildred Pierce. It was the role he would ultimately win the Academy Award for (Best Knee Pads). As I would listen to him upstairs, preparing, desperately trying to master the skates, wheeling madly down a corridor and smashing into a wall screaming, "Damn it!" I would think to myself, "Perhaps there is justice in this world, after all."

And so I remained cloistered in my basement world—while outside the music of the seventies filled the streets with hope and vision. I think perhaps Cat Stevens's tune "Tea for the Tillerman" said it best: "Bring Tea for the Tillerman, Steak for the sun, / Wine for the Women who made the rain come."

The Thumb-wrestle Miracle

It's almost as if that song were written for Daddy and me. It is really the perfect analogy for our relationship; Daddy was the Tillerman, tilling the soil under a hot sun. I was the Tea for the Tillerman, brought in to quench his thirst. I don't know who the Women were who "made the rain come," but you can be sure that the "Steak for the sun" was blood-rare, because Daddy was in charge, and that's the only way Daddy liked his steaks.

8/ Rebuttal to Chapter Seven

I TRUST THAT LAST CHAPTER IS IN keeping with the rest; I haven't had a chance to read it yet. Just as I was about to do so, I got a call from Harley Freeney, our local photographer, asking me to get down to the fish market. He's been hired by the publisher of this book to get some shots of me going about my business on the local scene.

Harley's a rather tight-lipped individual; we don't know much about his background, since he set up shop here a couple of years back. All he'll tell us is that before he took up photography he'd been an assistant computer-systems analyst for a major Midwest waste-water management company. Which give us little to go on.

While he snapped pictures of me pricing a pound of finnan haddie, I regaled him and the clerk with some of the thoughts I've had while driving the new car along I-95.

For example, do business places where they make you sign in but never sign out bug you like they do me?

Rebuttal to Chapter Seven

Wouldn't it have been great if Hollywood had had a Spurious Pictures Company? Its top star would have been Humphrey Bogus. . . . Are there any hillbillies around Bucharest, Romania? . . . Wonder if there's such a job as cymbal repairman. . . . Capers do not come from Canada. . . . Is the old saying "Warm winter—fat graveyards" really true? . . . Radio announcers in Maine only sound comfortable in their chosen profession when they're reading baseball scores. . . . Why hasn't somebody come up with a TV sitcom titled *The Greenfields of Vermont*? . . . Can roach dung cure cancer? . . . In commercials, all old women call servicemen, gas-station attendants, and supermarket clerks "Sonny." . . . Wonder if we've ever had a president who was a ventriloquist. . . . When I sit on a shoeshine stand, the guy sitting next to me always has on more expensive shoes than I do. . . . It seems like all the places you write to for nostalgia tapes of your favorite old-timers are in Minneapolis. . . . In Lincoln's day, could his mother have said, "Here, have a sandwich, Abe"? Or would she have just said "Here, have one of these"? . . . Was there ever a ballet dancer who chewed tobacco? . . . I never could see any resemblance between Candice Bergen and Charlie Mc-Carthy. . . . Longshoremen must sometimes get pier pressure. . . .

Harley and I finished with the fish man and drove across town to the dump, which he thought might be a good location for some gag shots. This, I thought, was a good time to spring a short quiz on him!

1. What's the only word in the English language with three consecutive dotted letters?

2. What's the name of that dent between your upper lip and your nose?
3. How many plays did Shakespeare write?

(The answers somewhere ahead.)

As long as we're into this kind of stuff, this might be the place to use my "I've read somewhere that . . ." collection.
For instance:

I've read somewhere that: In the cemetery monument trade, those small vertical marble markers for graves are called "fireplugs." . . . A sweater is often called a jersey because it was worn by sailors of the Island of Jersey in the English Channel. . . . Crickets chirp faster in warm weather, slower when it's cold. The temperature is roughly equal to the number of chirps you hear in fifteen seconds, plus thirty-seven. . . . In almost all small towns the local cop on the beat always has a key to the gas station. . . . There's a piece of airport equipment called a "scissors manlift." . . . The study of cross-eyedness is strabismology. . . . Over 100 million toothpicks are made in Maine every day.

It's only a rumor but: The Corgi people are recalling all their 1982 cars because of steering defects. . . . Martex is putting out a line of towels with "Its" on them. . . . There's an Eerieview Asylum in Cleveland. . . . There's a pair of lawyers in Chicago named Brusque and Curt. . . . and in San Diego a law firm called Perfidia,

Frenesi and Perdido." . . . Lawrence Welk will
make a comeback with a hit record called "The
Edgar Allan Polka." . . . The latest sitcom on
Tibetan television is *I Remember Llama.*

I can't believe they really said that in a commercial:

HOUSEWIFE: "I've switched my loyalty from the
leading bottled Italian dressing."

HUSBAND: "Don't I get fresh-squeezed orange
juice on my birthday?"
WIFE: "But, dear, you like the leading
brand of frozen concentrate."

LADY EXEC: "I take it as directed and consult my
doctor if pain persists."

And I'm waiting for this:

MAN TO DRUGGIST: "It's hemorrhoids, Doc. I need
something to—you know—relieve the temporary itching, mild pain, and irritation due to
minor inflammation, for use only as prescribed!"

Uses for our old friend, shellac:

Dipping a screw in thinned shellac before putting it into wood will keep it from rusting.

You can keep your cookbook covers fresh-looking by applying a coat of transparent shellac.

Equal amounts of light shellac and alcohol applied thinly will give renewed life to limp straw hats.

We'd finished the pictures and Harley was packing up his equipment. I thanked him for his time and promised to send him a copy of the book when it comes out, but he wouldn't leave until I gave him the

ANSWERS TO THE QUIZ

1. Hijinks
2. Philtrum
3. Thirty-seven.

9/ "Never Forget Daddy's Day!"

UMMMM, I DIDN'T KNOW ALL THAT stuff about shellac. That was kind of interesting. Ummm, well, anyway . . .

The additional eight hundred or so pounds I'd gained in my adolescence contributed to an ever-increasing insecurity about the outside world, and I began to withdraw from everyone and everything around me: family, friends, pets, servants, flowers, bugs, even single-celled life-forms. In fact, once I remember Daddy bounding into my room holding something in his cupped palms. "Hey, Chris, I've got a handful of single-celled life-forms!" he announced, "You want some?" I screamed and told him, "Keep the damn things away from me," and then I waddled away as fast as my elephant legs would carry me, leaving Daddy a little more than just baffled; "Gee, I wonder what crawled up *his* flue?"

I wanted to be alone. I wanted to fade away, to curl up and disappear, perhaps even to die, to eat myself to death . . . to eat and eat and eat until I exploded into a thousand points of light.

Daddy's Boy

On my sixteenth birthday I climbed into my bed. I covered my blubberous body with a huge tarp, lent to us by the grounds keeper at Shea Stadium, braided my hair, and vowed never, ever to get out of bed again! That was my plan. I would stay in bed forever or until whatever was going to happen . . . happened.

The entire Elliott Clan was embarrassed. At first Daddy didn't take me seriously. "Hey, Chris," he said teasingly, "if you get out of bed, I'll buy you a Dunkin' Donuts franchise!" But all his valiant efforts were met with failure. My mind was made up. I would not budge. As time wore on, I think the reality and severity of my situation sunk in with Daddy, but still the whole thing never threw him the way I was hoping it would. I think he liked knowing where I was at all times. He liked the fact that I was no longer challenging him, that I was no longer a threat to him, and he was also making a bundle charging six bucks a pop to family friends who were curious to view his amazing eight-hundred-pound Elephant Boy.

All my needs were seen to. Each day the servants arrived with the tons of food I required, tutors from Herbert kept me up-to-date with my classes, and the fellas from the car wash bathed me. I passed the time watching my stories on TV, embroidering pillows with happy faces or slogans like "Keep on truckin'," and reading the works of the great spiritual leaders of the world. I became spiritually "enlightened," and I was convinced that Maher Baba had been reincarnated as Francesco Rinaldi from the spaghetti-sauce commercials. And the longer I stayed in bed, the more famous I became. I was a sort of local celebrity. GIANT BOY SCARES THE HELL OUT OF US! proclaimed a tabloid, and in the text it read, ". . . women are known to shriek and faint at the mere sight of him, for he is that hideous!" I didn't mind such exaggerations, because I was becoming a star. So in bed I stayed. I stayed there for two straight years.

The more publicity I generated, the larger the curious crowds grew outside the Hut, and eventually Daddy opened his freak exhibit to the public. I gave six shows daily and enjoyed the attention. I didn't realize it, but I was subconsciously killing myself, subconsciously checking out, and subconsciously trying to get under Daddy's skin and really rattle him, but I don't think I ever succeeded. One person who realized I was "on my way out the door" was funnyman Dick Gregory. Mr. Gregory had been a longtime friend of the Elliott Clan, and when he saw the condition I was in, he immediately prescribed his Bahamian Diet. In just four months I lost enough weight to be able to roll over on my side without the help of the pulley system we had installed. I couldn't thank him enough. Before I knew it, I was up and around and able to face the outside world.

To this day I know Daddy was irked that he was not the one to cure me of my obesity, that someone else had succeeded where he had failed, and that his deal with Ringling Brothers had fallen through, but those were his problems. I just thanked God for Dick Gregory. If it had not been for him, I would not be here today, nor would I have written *Daddy's Boy: A Son's Shocking Account of Life with a Famous Father* and *My Search for Elvis*, so I feel that the entire literary community owes a big "Thank you, Dick!" to Mr. Dick Gregory.

The pounds dropped off and I continued to slim down, and gradually a new Chris Elliott emerged. I was becoming beautiful beyond compare. My weight leveled off at one hundred and fifty pounds, and there, before me in the mirror, stood a six-foot-two, eighteen-year-old Adonis with a mane of thick, wheat-colored hair, dreamy blue eyes, and a chin just like Mike Douglas's.

Daddy was completely intimidated by "the new me." He was quite surprised that I had emerged from my shell of blubber such a "looker," and he avoided me at all costs. He hid from me in the Hut, and the only time we were together, at dinner, he insisted on crossing his eyes so he wouldn't have to look at me straight. It was obvious he was jealous of my beauty. (By the way, did I say my chin was like Mike Douglas's? Sorry, I meant *Kirk* Douglas.)

Daddy's relationship with me had changed. He was envious of the wide-open future ahead of me, and full of regrets for the heavy past he dragged behind him. I was no longer his little Daddy's Boy. He now saw me as a cocky punk, speeding along in a souped-up hot rod, about to overtake him on the highway of fame and fortune. Could it be that the tables were turning? If there was any question, Daddy made it perfectly clear that he was still in control, that he was still pulling the strings, still orchestrating my emotions, still Mr. Big Cheese, the day I graduated from high school.

My graduation from Herbert was to be a significant event in the early dawn of adulthood that I was now embracing. I saw my graduation as my final ascent into manhood, a razor-sharp sword to slash away the tethers of adolescence, a ticker-tape parade declaring victory in the war against my upbringing, and, most importantly, the opportunity for Daddy to heal some wounds by buying me a really expensive graduation present. (I was hoping for two cars.)

I was the last "thug" to pass through the hallowed halls of Herbert. My older brothers had already graduated, already gone to college, and for the most part were all embarking on promising careers; Bob, Jrs., Numbers One and Two were in business together manufacturing Gentlemen's Hanky Dryers, which were little clothes dryers that a gentleman would keep in his back pocket (after he used his handkerchief, he would throw the wet rag in the dryer and in no time the cloth was as good as new). They were selling like hotcakes, and plans for a stackable washer-and-dryer system were already in the works. Numbers Three and Four were doing very well selling real estate that simply did not exist. Somehow they had convinced a number of people that all the mapmakers of the world were wrong and that there was still a huge stretch of uncharted land extending east from Key West, Florida, at a forty-five-degree angle, in the shape of a big, hairy monster. Thousands of rugged pioneer families dumped their life savings into acres and acres of this invisible property, and headed south to start over in the land called the New Frontier. The twins, A and B, shaved their heads, moved to Iran, and opened a chain of Bob's Big Boys, and the rest of the thugs were at

Stanford Medical School trying to come up with a cure for those obnoxious people who insist on closing their eyes whenever they talk. So I had a lot to live up to.

I looked forward to my graduation day with heightened anticipation. Finally Daddy would have to bear witness to my own solo achievement. I couldn't wait to see his face when I received my diploma. It would be a moment of triumph that even he could not steal. As with everything else at Herbert, the commencement ceremony was held outside. It was a very warm, crystal-clear early June day in 1978. The sidewalk between Sixty-seventh and Sixty-eighth Street was lined with parents and friends, and I remember gathering with my classmates in our caps and gowns, organizing ourselves into a line, and preparing to parade up the block to the platform on Sixty-eighth Street where the ceremony's guest speaker and our diplomas awaited. All my classmates remarked on how beautiful I looked, and I thanked them politely. As we readied ourselves, I canvassed the crowd. I could see my mother, and I could see my brothers, but I could not see Daddy.

The band struck up "Pomp and Circumstance" and we began to march up the street. Occasionally a proud parent would pop a flashbulb, give a thumbs-up, or blow a kiss; and I kept waiting for Daddy to jump out and say, "Say cheese!" but he never did. I couldn't help thinking that after experiencing such a horrible and shocking upbringing, perhaps the graduation would be a vindication of sorts. Perhaps afterward Daddy and I might deal with each other on equal turf. Perhaps after graduation Daddy would embrace me, not just as an extension of himself but as another human being; and perhaps after graduation he would give me the passbook to a six-million-dollar trust fund. The prospects were enchanting and I was excited.

About three quarters of the way up the street, old Uncle Sid broke through the crowd, rushed up to me, and shoved a big brown envelope into my hands. "Your Daddy wanted you to have this, ummmmm," he said breathlessly. "And by the way, you are looking very handsome, ummmmm!" And then he was consumed by the crowd. As we marched on toward the platform I opened the note attached to the envelope and read it.

Dear Daddy's Boy,
Sorry old chum, but I cannot make it to your graduation from high school. Believe me, I know how important this day is in your life. I know how exciting the prospect of entering the world must be for you, and I realize how much you wanted me there to experience this moment with you, but alas, I'm due to get those annoying hairs on the back of my neck trimmed, and Jerry the Barber claims he can't move my appointment! Such is luck, eh?

As always, fondly,
Your father,
Bob Elliott

P.S. Please accept the enclosed, delicious Tom Carvel Ice Cream Cake, as a token of my congratulations on this, your graduation day!

This was the final blow. How could he do this to me? I looked into the brown envelope, and the ice-cream cake, which Daddy must have squooshed inside, was no more. It had melted in the June sun and was nothing more than a blob. My best guess was that in an earlier life it had been a Cookie-O'Puss.

So there I was, ascending the platform, about to receive my high school diploma and step out into the world a man, and yet I was bawling like an infant. Daddy was not there. He couldn't make it. He had to get his neck hair trimmed! What hurt the most was that I was fully aware, and Daddy knew I was fully aware, that Jerry's Barbershop was located on Sixty-eighth Street between Park and Lexington. It was the ultimate insult, not only to skip my graduation but also to make me aware that he was no more than thirty feet away at the time!

He had succeeded in ruining the one day in my life that I looked forward to. I sat on the platform with my classmates, barely aware of the proceedings, trying to quiet the flood of tears. I tried to regain my composure but I could not. I don't remember much, as everything was overshadowed by Daddy's incredible stunt. I know my class had booked Ralph Nader to be the guest speaker, but he had backed out at the last minute and we ended up with character actor Marlon Brando. All I remember was Marlon wearing a dress, droning on and on for two and a half hours on how just because we've graduated high school, we shouldn't think that we don't have to wash anymore.

I felt myself sinking deep into the scum-laden sludge of the contaminated swamp of my life.

The day was one big anticlimactic thud. There were no big parties, no big presents, no cars, no six-million-dollar trust fund—only a melted ice-cream cake. I saw hide nor hair of Daddy that night. He hid from me, and the next morning I left for Upstate New York and my first real job. It was the summer that would change my life.

Thanks to Uncle Sid's connections, I secured a position as an apprentice at the Ole Mill House Summer Stock Theater in Woodstock, New York. I didn't see Daddy at all during the summer of 1978. He was busy directing a miniseries for television about his life, starring Richard Chamberlain as him (the perfect choice for the role). Somehow I knew when I returned that things would be different, but I didn't care; I just wanted to strike out on my own, take my first plunge into show business, and make my own big splash.

The Ole Mill House Theater was an Equity stage, which meant it played host to all the big national tours that were traveling around that summer. We opened the season with *Oliver!* starring little Ricky Schroeder in the title role and Charlie Callas as Fagin. Next was a musical drama entitled *Dance, You Mother!* starring Tommy Tune and Richard Roundtree. The all-dog version of *The Odd Couple* opened in mid-season and was the only production not very well received, basically because the dog trainers had to remain onstage throughout the entire play and the action became confusing with all these guys running around the set with whips. The next to last show was a heavy four-act drama by Eugene O'Neill called *When the Cherry Blossoms Stink Up the Lawn,* and it starred Jason Robards, Colleen Dewhurst, and Geraldine Fitzgerald. Finally the season finished up with *Jesus Christ, Superstar,* with old family pal Dick Cavett in the starring role. I was looking forward to that show; I hadn't seen Mr. Cavett since my tenth birthday party, and I was eager to see his disappearing-cigarette trick again.

My duties as apprentice were as varied as the productions that we were mounting. There were ten apprentices all together, and we were the lowest of the low on the totem pole. I thought for sure my good looks and the Elliott name would excuse me from the most horrid and lowly tasks, but no such luck. The theater was run by a married Lesbian couple named Bill and Wendy Roberts, and the first day I arrived Bill made it perfectly clear that there would be no special privileges for Daddy's Boy, even though I was the most beautiful man she had ever seen. I didn't mind the work so much. Somehow I felt like I was paying my dues, learning my trade, and cutting my teeth.

In exchange for the long hours and hard labor, Bill and Wendy supplied the apprentices with room and board and a ten-dollar-a-week stipend. In addition, professionals "in the business" would come up to the Ole Mill House and hold encouraging seminars on theater and show business.

One weekend the great acting coach Lee Strasberg arrived at the Ole Mill House and held a three-day acting workshop. I was so thrilled and excited; truly, everyone was. This was the event of the summer, and no apprentice would miss the opportunity to learn some secrets of the trade from the master. We all gathered in the rehearsal barn. "You must learn to be what you are not," he told us. "Think of what you are, and then you must determine what you are not, then, if you can, take what you are not and jam it into what you are, and then . . . make it your own!"

I was completely baffled. I hadn't understood a word he said, but I was still intrigued and in awe of the great Lee Strasberg.

He called Bartley Flash up to the center of the barn. Bartley was a nice enough guy, but a little on the heavy side and given to massive perspiration attacks. "Be a bicycle!" commanded Mr. Strasberg, and Bartley was stunned. He had no idea where to begin. It was a pathetic scene to watch. First Bartley got down on his hands and knees, then he started to flail his arms about in a desperate attempt to depict wheels, then he made a honk-honk sound like the Road Runner. It was terribly sad, but I laughed out loud at poor Bartley just as the rest of his audience did. Despite the miserable performance, I still feel that Strasberg laid into him a little too heavily.

"What the hell are you doing? You call that a bicycle? That's no bicycle! That's a fat kid who wants to be an actor acting like an imbecile!"

There was a puddle of sweat on the floor at Flash's feet, and Strasberg made him spend the rest of the class standing in the corner with his pants down, sucking his thumb. "Gosh," I thought to myself, "did Daddy have to go through this kind of humiliation?" Strasberg was being unduly harsh with poor Bartley, but then again, Strasberg was a genius, and he must have known what was best for the fat apprentice. Still, the rest of us sat trembling in our seats at the dreadful prospect of being called up in front of the class.

"Mr. Elliott, let us have you come to the center of the room!"

His words were laced with heavy sarcasm and

peppered with a dash of nastiness. "Oh, God, no, not me!" I thought to myself. "Please don't let me fail, please don't let me fail!"

"So you are Chris Elliott, son of the Great Bob Elliott—Daddy's Boy, they call you?"

"Yes, sir," I said, trembling like the Cowardly Lion.

"I'm quite familiar with your father's work. In fact, I happen to be a big fan."

"Thank you, sir, I know he's a big fan of—"

"Quiet!" he demanded. "I'm not through speaking." He paused, zeroing in on my knocking knees. "Well, let us see if Daddy's Boy has inherited his father's talent. Let us see if Daddy's Boy has more going for him besides his incredible good looks, shall we? And so . . . Daddy's Boy, be a bicycle!"

No, no, not that! Yes, I had laughed at poor Bartley, and yes, I thought his performance was idiotic, but I never said that I could do better myself! I had no more of a grasp on the exercise than poor old Flash. What was I going to do? Anything other than a bicycle: a banana, a mouse, a bowl of soup, anything! I simply had no idea how to *be* a bicycle. I knew I was about to fail. In front of me, the faces of my nine fellow apprentices symbolically transformed into Daddy's face. The face I had seen all my life. The face daring me to fail, leading me into constant successlessness, down the path into total abandonment. Then, for some reason, the nine faces in front of me transformed from Daddy's face into Alan Alda's face. I still don't know why.

At any rate, I suddenly snapped out of my emotional free-fall, filled my soul with confidence, and told myself, "You are a bicycle, you are, you are, you

are a bicycle!" Quickly I flashed back to my childhood . . . to the red Stingray with raised handlebars
and banana seat; I concentrated, I pictured every
detail on every inch of the bicycle clearly and suc-
cinctly in my mind . . . and then, like magic, I became that bicycle!

I don't know how I did it. I don't know what inner
power I had tapped into, but I had truly—physically
and literally—become that bicycle. In fact,
Strasberg took a Polaroid of me during the exercise,
but the photo did not show a human being; instead,
clearly visible in the center of the room, was the red
Stingray with raised handlebars and banana seat. I
heard later that there had been some concern because I remained in the form of a bicycle for ten
minutes, and the apprentices were taking turns riding me around the room trying to get me to snap out
of it. Eventually I did snap out of it, and when the
applause in the room died down, Strasberg approached me, put his hand on my shoulder, and said,
"Now *that* was a bicycle!"

The incident changed my life. I knew I was a capable actor. I knew I had inherited Daddy's talents
and that I could be a star if I wanted to be. I had
proven myself to my peers, and I had gained respect.
I showed everyone that I was more than just a handsome, privileged rich kid; I showed them that I was a
genius as well. If only Daddy had been there to see
me in action.

The rest of the summer was not the same. I
changed. I was full of myself. I turned my nose up at
hard labor and neglected my duties, mouthing off
that I was too good to get my hands dirty. I called

Uncle Sid ten times a day, imploring him to set up gigs for me upon my return to the city in the fall. Bill tried to straighten me out. "Listen, kid, you got a lot of folks around here thinking you're a bit of a snob, you know what I mean?" she said. "Yeah, I know, Bill, I'll try to do better," I promised, feigning humility. "Thattaboy!" she said, and as I turned to walk away she gave me a hard smack on the butt.

There was nothing anyone could say or do to bring me around to my senses. I truly believed that I was a star and as such, I deserved to be treated differently (another talent I obviously inherited). I had not heard from or spoken to Daddy the entire summer. We had not corresponded, and that was fine with me. Still, I couldn't wait to return home and compete with him in the glamorous world of show business. For the time being, college was out; after all, I had my big career to get rolling.

Jesus Christ Superstar, the last show of the season, opened, and Dick Cavett was actually very good as the Savior, and he brought down the house each night with the "Thieves in the Temple" number.

My assignment for the last show was to be Mr. Cavett's dresser, a job I was happy to take on, considering the fact that the man had watched me grow up. I remember one night Dick had just finished dressing and there were still ten minutes to curtain, so we stepped outside behind the theater for some fresh air. It was dusk, and although it was only late August, the air was flavored with a distinct autumn cool. We talked about the good old days, about the big birthday parties at Fox Run, about the glory years of Manhattan, and about his fond memories of

Groucho Marx. Then he went off on a tangent and started talking about peanut butter again, and I had to bring him back to more pertinent conversation.

"Two minutes, Mr. Cavett!" called the stage manager, and we started to head back into the theater; but Dick paused and turned to me thoughtfully. "Have you heard from your daddy this summer?" he asked.

"No, not a word."

"Umm, that doesn't surprise me," he said. "He's hurt that you didn't send him a Daddy's Day card! Well, excuse me, I have to go get into my character now."

My head suddenly felt numb all over, like it was inside a giant ice cube. He was right. I had forgotten to send Daddy a Daddy's Day card. (Father's Day was always referred to as Daddy's Day in our family.) How could I have done such a thing? How could I have been so thoughtless? Wait a second, the guy didn't even show up at my high school graduation! Why should I feel guilty? Nah, it made no difference what had passed between us before; *you just don't forget Daddy's Day!* I rushed to my room at Bill and Wendy's house and dashed off a note as fast as I could:

Dear Daddy,
Happy Daddy's Day!

       Yours always,
       Daddy's Boy

I backdated the note, and through Uncle Sid's contacts at the post office I was able to bribe a mailman to deliver the note promptly and to take the blame for misplacing it in the first place. It was the perfect solution, the Elliott ingenuity at work. Shortly before I was to return home, I received this rather curt letter from Daddy:

Dear Daddy's Boy,
Thank you for your kind Daddy's Day card. It meant a great deal to me, but you cast the wrong mailman in the role of "stooge." Upon delivery, he immediately broke down and told the whole story, how you bribed him to take the blame, etc., etc. I must say, you are a chip off the old block. Nonetheless, Daddy's Boy, I am bitterly upset that you forgot my favorite holiday in the first place. Perhaps next year your memory will serve you better.

Now, since you are due to return in a fortnight, I feel obliged to apprise you of some developments that have occurred in your absence. Since your brothers are all off making successes of themselves, your mother and I felt that the Hut was too much for us to handle, and so we have sold it. I understand that it is to be made into a museum. Your mother and I now reside in the penthouse suite down at Bob's Big Towers. It is my opinion that immediately upon your return you should seek accommodations elsewhere, for you are now old enough to be out on your own, and there is just no room for you in the lavish, forty-room penthouse where we now live.

Fondly,
Your father,
Bob Elliott

An era had truly passed. The Hut was gone, and with it the sights and sounds of my childhood. I had no idea what to expect when I returned to Manhattan. Things were definitely changing.

The penthouse apartment that Daddy wrote about was located on the 106th floor of the office complex that he'd built downtown in the early seventies. Bob's Big Towers consisted of two chimneylike sky- scrapers, each 106 stories tall. It was the center for international trade and the tallest pair of buildings in all of Manhattan. I felt the layout of the grand apartment was rather awkward; it occupied both top floors in both buildings, but there was no bridge connecting the two areas. The bedrooms and dining room sat atop one tower, while the living room and kitchen sat atop the other. If you wanted a midnight snack, you had no recourse but to take the elevator all the way down to the first floor, cross outside into the other building, and take the elevator all the way back up to the 106th floor where the kitchen was. It was terribly inconvenient, so I was not upset that Daddy wanted me to live somewhere else.

When I returned to New York in early September, I immediately set out to find the perfect bachelor pad. I signed a lease for a one-room flat above a garage up on 129th Street and Adam Clayton Powell Boulevard. It was all I could afford, as Daddy had cut off all my allowance, but it was home.

No sooner had I settled into my pad than the door flew open and a parade of deliverymen marched in carrying giant boxes marked FRAGILE. Box after box was brought in and stacked in my tiny apartment. "What the hell is all of this?" I inquired.

"Housewarming present . . . from your dad."

Then I knew exactly what was inside each box. I signed for the delivery and sat in the middle of the room, surrounded by the crates. It was his dumb Beam bottle collection. Daddy always thought I wanted his Beam bottle collection, and yet I had no room even to unpack it. In fact, now I had no room for furniture. Daddy's Beam bottle collection would remain in its boxes and serve as my sofa and chairs.

I got very little work acting. It was a humbling experience. I had returned from the Ole Mill Theater feeling like a hotshot, ready to take on the Big Apple, but I found a million other young actors who were more talented than me, better equipped than me, with their own handbags and leg warmers, competing for the same roles as me. Poor Uncle Sid, bless his heart, was now well into his hundreds and had lost a good many of his "in" connections. The only steady gig he could find me was some street-mime work in front of what is now called the Metropolitan Museum of Art. I couldn't be choosy. I grabbed it.

The irony of it all was so thick that you could cut it with a knife. There I was, in front of Fox Run, the Hut, my old home, dressed in black leotards, my face covered in clown-white makeup, dancing around like an idiot. I may have been able to turn myself into a bicycle for Lee Strasberg, but I was a lousy mime. Spectators actually threw garbage at me when I did the trapped-in-a-box routine. It was hell all over again. I was embarrassed; it was the same utter humiliation that I felt back when I was a child visiting Santa Claus at Macy's. I was failing again. Failing, failing, failing. But now, in front of the eyes of the stately Hut, I could hear its stone steps shrieking in that shrill, high-pitched voice: "You stink! You'll never be like your Daddy. You stink!"

Many years went by. I had lost touch with my

family, dabbled in different careers, been through six divorces, and was not in the best of moods. The odor emanating from the swamp of my life was so foul, you needed a gas mask just to breathe.

Then one day a messenger arrived with a gold-embossed invitation to the Broadway opening of *Bob-O-Mania*, a musical tribute to Bob Elliott (with a number of actors portraying him at various stages in his life). It was obvious to me that Daddy's career had moved into a different realm. He was not performing anymore but still remained in the public eye, and by promoting made-for-TV movies about his life, Broadway musicals celebrating his contributions, one-man shows detailing his history, autobiographies mixing fact with fiction, and Halloween costumes depicting his likeness, he created the illusion of being very active in "the business." But then again, who was I to talk? The last real acting job I had was playing McGruff the Crime Dog at a mall in Paramus.

Opening night was as grand an affair as you can imagine. Thousands of Bob Elliott fans jammed the streets on either side of the Winter Garden Theater. Many of them were wearing "bald wigs," in honor of their idol. One by one, long black limousines pulled up, depositing their celebrities onto the red carpet. It was a scene that invoked images of old Manhattan. When Uncle Sid and I got out of our limo, there was only a small smattering of applause, and someone said, "Hey, it's Daddy's Boy!" and someone else said, "Who cares?"

Uncle Sid squeezed my arm and tried to comfort me. "Don't you worry about it, kid, you'll show them all, ummmmmmm." But I no longer believed him. My time had passed.

Bob-O-Mania was not bad at all. It was very well done. The guy who played young Bob Elliott was pretty good, but the guy who played older Bob Elliott looked more like Yasir Arafat.

Afterward the opening-night party was held in the penthouse suite at Bob's Big Towers and it was another huge, glitzy event, and another reminder of the good old days. Everyone was there, all the old gang, and there was no getting close to Bob Elliott. He was constantly surrounded by friends, groupies, and secret service men. It was nice to see Mother and all my brothers again, but everyone was doing so well and making a point of telling me how well they were doing that I became extremely depressed. I started to slam down the drinks one after another. "Rob Roys! Rob Roys! More Rob Roys!" It was the first time in my life that I had gotten completely smashed. I had never had more than two or three drinks in my life (because I am *not* an *alcoholic*!), but that night I got completely ossified.

At about three in the morning, with the party still going strong, I made my way up to the roof. It was cold and windy. I wasn't sure why I was about to do what I was about to do, but I did it, anyway. I strung a heavy cable between the two glass towers, snapped down a lightning rod to use as a balancing pole, and stepped out onto the cable.

I had never tightrope-walked in my life, but the alcohol in my system filled me with daredevil confidence. I was sure I could do anything. So there I was, one hundred and six stories above the pavement, balancing on a one-inch-thick cable. Surely I would die this time. If, indeed, I had a death wish, it would most certainly come true that night, wouldn't it? I walked to the center of the line and stood, swaying in the wind. I was drunk and I was dizzy, and the Manhattan skyline and the black sky, dotted with a thousand points of light, swirled around me like a never-ending kaleidoscope. Why was I out there? Why did I want to die? It was my final call to be noticed, my final plea to be my own man, and it was the stupidest thing I had ever done in my life. With the balancing rod held tightly in my left hand, I reached into my pocket with my right hand and pulled out old Uncle Sid's lucky shot glass from Atlantic City. I had kept the souvenir with me at all times ever since the *Andrea Doria* incident. Now I held the glass out in front of me, smirking at its supposed good luck, and in a last act of defiance I opened my hand and committed the "memento" to the atmosphere. It plummeted down, and in the hollow quietness of the city I heard a faint shatter, one hundred and six stories below me. My luck had run out!

It took a while before a few partygoers looked out the window and noticed me suspended in midair . . . and then I blacked out.

When I woke, Daddy was pouring black coffee down my throat. "Of all the dumb, crazy, harebrained stunts you've ever pulled, this one has to take the cake!"

"I'm alive?" I asked.

"Yes, you're alive, you're just drunk!"

"How did I get down?"

"I got you down, you little brat! You forget that your Daddy *started* his career in the circus. It's lucky for you I still had my tights and slippers around!"

"I'm sorry I ruined your party, Daddy," I said as I got up to leave. Daddy may have saved my life, but I could tell by the tone in his voice that he didn't want me overstaying my welcome.

"Where do you think you're going?" he asked.

"I'm gonna grab a subway up to 129th Street and Adam Clayton Powell Boulevard!"

I had one foot out the door when I heard Daddy mumble, "You can stay here tonight, if you like. There's room on the sofa."

I was stunned. He was offering me a place to stay for the night. He was doing something kind, something thoughtful, and for a moment I had no idea how to react.

"You're asking me to stay?"

"Yeah, stay! Stay on the sofa, go ahead!"

Was this Daddy? *My* Daddy? If he *were* the same person, was he trying to turn over a new leaf? Did he think he could suddenly heal all the old wounds? I was faced with a dilemma. Should I take a chance? Should I spend the night on the sofa and tomorrow begin to rebuild my relationship with my father? Or was it too late to rebuild . . . to heal, to forgive and forget, to start over? And would Daddy just go back to his old ways in the morning?

Then, like a bolt of lightning, I was filled with resolve and was certain what my course would be.

"No thank you," I said, "I have my own place uptown," and I turned to leave.

"Hey, kid!" Daddy said, halting my exit. "You

know, you weren't the worst Daddy's Boy in the world!" I was touched. "You weren't the worst Daddy," I replied, "although there were times when . . . nah, forget it." I didn't want to ruin the moment.

"So what will you do now?" he asked.

"What I always do . . . survive! I'm a survivor, Daddy. That was the one thing you never counted on: that I could survive, that I could find the inner strength to battle every obstacle and win. It's what I've had to do all my life, and it's what I'll continue to do till the day I die. You see, Daddy, all the days of my life have been eclipsed by your long shadow, overcast by your cloudbursts that showered down upon me billions of hard, jagged rocks, and any umbrella that I tried to seek shelter beneath was useless because the detritus that you were dropping on me came plummeting down too fast, and it ripped through the nylon, shredding all my umbrellas to rags. But all that is going to change now. From here on in I'm my own man. I'm my own master, my own column to lean on, and from now on I'm not walking in anybody's shadow but my own. What do you think of that, fella?"

Daddy stared blankly at me for a moment and then said, "I'm sorry, I wasn't listening. What did you say?"

"Forget it. It was nothing. Good-bye, Daddy!" and I exited.

Once the door to the penthouse apartment shut, Daddy remained still and silent for a moment, but then a solitary tear rolled down his cheek. He knew I was gone, and he whispered, "Good-bye, my son." (I'm not sure if that really happened, because I wasn't in the room, but I would imagine that something a lot like that happened.)

The elevator made its descent slower than I wanted it to. I couldn't get away fast enough. I was finally and forever free. (Until the nightmares started back up and I had to write this book to purge myself of my horrifying past.) Yes, I was free of Daddy, free of his grasp; and if I chose, I would never have to hear his demanding voice again.

Suddenly the elevator filled with the familiar baritone of Bob Elliott. His voice was emanating from the speaker on the push-button panel, and I could tell he was choked up.

"Chris," he said, "I know you can hear me. I just want to say something to you. You can leave now. You can walk out; you have a right to . . . to start over. But please, no matter where you go, no matter how far away you travel, even if you never, ever see me again . . . please . . . never forget Daddy's Day!"

The elevator door opened and I rushed out into the cold blackness of early morning. The first piercing red beams of the rising sun silhouetted the skyline of the great metropolis, and I turned my collar to the cool morning wind. As I headed uptown I realized that I was eager to begin doing what we all do once the devastating storm has passed: We start over!

10/ Rebuttal to Chapter Nine

I HAVE JUST ASCERTAINED THAT Arthur Godfrey did not record "Teterboro Tower" the year my son was born. This is an excellent example of just how much careful research goes into books like this.

Further research suggests that eight out of ten who read this don't remember the old redhead, anyway.

It should also be mentioned that portions of the original manuscript for Chapter Eight were effectively mangled by our schnauzer, Moxie, and had to be rewritten from memory. I don't recall exactly what material those first pages contained, but Moxie seemed to enjoy them.

The weather has turned cool now. I've tried to summon up the enthusiasm to resume thinking about the festival, but somehow the idea has lost its original appeal.

Even the discovery of this little-known, yellowed poem under a stack of Jerry Vale records in the back closet has left me with little to bet major money on.

Daddy's Boy

The Haddock Thinks
He's Better Than the Cod

The haddock is often quite snooty
   To the cod in the depths of the sea.
It's not that he thinks he's a beauty:
   It's what he calls his destiny.

It began off of Scotland, oh long years ago,
   When they caught him and brought him ashore,
They washed and they cleaned him above and below,
   And smoked him then smoked him some more.

In the land where golf started somewhere on a dune
   And there came into being the caddie,
Smoked haddock became widely known very soon
   And they gave it the name finnan haddie.

So the haddock feels he's a superior fish,
   Though the cod takes of this a dim view.
For smoked cod, when it's cooked, is as tasty a dish:
   Finnan could be his given name too.

Thus the codfish's nose is a bit out of joint.
   While the haddock looks right down his snout.
There's no way that I know of to show them the point:
   They're equals. Let them argue it out.

Labor Day weekend came and went; cars poured out of the state through the Kittery tollbooths at the rate of thirty-five hundred an hour.

We spent the holiday in much the same way we had for years: turning on television the first thing in the morning to see how much Jerry had raised overnight.

"Thanks so much, Telly, for being here," he'd be saying to the departing Telly Savalas. "My gratitude was only exceeded by my inability to expound on it!"

"Now, ladies and gentlemen, the forerunner of great entertainment, Danny Thomas!"

About mid-morning, it's our routine to drive into town and take in the always anticipated festivities on the green around the Blue Barron Memorial Bandstand.

For the kids there are potato-sack races, face-painting experts, and stilt walkers. Among the diverse adult entertainments, the annual Geriatric Olympics, highlights of which are the bean-bag throw, the seventy-five-foot walk, and the wheelchair relay race.

Each year I contribute my part to the day by leading the community sing, since I'm about the only one available who has any show-business experience.

To get the crowd's attention, I shout: "Hey, senior citizens! What time is it?"

And they shout back: "It's oat-bran muffin time!"

From then on the fun's guaranteed, especially with the help I get from Harley Freeney on the bandstand piano.

Back home, the Spinners have just concluded their appearance on the telethon, and Jerry is waving them good-bye.

"The Spinners, ladies and gentlemen! Let's have a nice hand—and take them off with a reception."

"Now, one of the infinitely foremost entertainers in the show-business syndrome. A terrific voice and an ultimately great talent, Sarah Vaughan!"

Jerry is tired.

I'm tired, too, I realize, as I return to my deck and

the view of Halfway Rock. The heron gulls still float against the sky, the sea has turned gray-green, and the air snaps with the crisp crackle of fall.

The book has certainly made for an interesting summer, even if it has forced postponement of the finnan haddie idea, probably forever. (Maybe a Toothpick Festival would be more appropriate?)

It's been a while since I've heard from Chris, and I suspect I'll be getting a get-rid-of-the-guilt call any minute, explaining he never thought his shocking story of growing up as the son of a famous star would take this long to write.

Someday, perhaps, I'll write my *own* book, and tell it like it really was. Then it'll be up to him to dream up answers to my "accusations"!

Right now I think I'll go out and try to buy a new mustache comb. I seem to have misplaced my old one.

Epilogue

I HAVE NOT CORRESPONDED WITH my father for quite some time now (actually, ever since I read some of his rebuttals in my publisher's office a few weeks ago), and so I have decided perhaps it would be appropriate to end my shocking account of life with a famous father with this little epistle to the Big Cheese himself:

Dear Daddy,

So here it is—the horrifying story that so desperately needed telling—perhaps not as *you* remember it, but instead the way it *really* happened . . . the way *I* remember it. *You're* the one who's got his facts a little mixed up! After all, *I* haven't been up in Maine all summer eating poison lobsters!

Perhaps this book will finally send a signal to you that I have come of age, that *I've grabbed my life by the horns,* that *I'm going my own way,* that *Little Chrissy is happy at last.* (By the way, those three clichés are other possible titles for the book. Let me know what you think of them.)

The question most likely to be raised upon publication of this work will be: Did I really have enough to complain about? I don't know the answer to that question. I only know that my rough manuscript exceeded (by thirty pages) the required one hundred and twenty pages that the publisher was vehemently demanding.

So, after all is said and done, life will go on. Someone told me that you have signed to write a movie for Spielberg; *Indiana Jones and the Chestful of Gold-Toe Socks*. I can only wish you well, Daddy. I'm sure it will be another big success for you, as you succeed with everything in life.

I am doing fine. My hair transplant and eye job have given me a fresh outlook on life, and I am a survivor. As you know, after twelve tumultuous marriages (the worst being to character actress Kaye Ballard), I am now finally happy and certain that I will not impose on my sons (Chris, Jrs., One through Five) the kinds of impositions that you imposed on me!

Still, I'm certain I will always remain a little like you, Daddy . . . a little arrogant . . . a little self-centered . . . but I'm not gonna let that bother me. I'm gonna go on living and never look back, because I know that there is one major thing that I do differently from you and which will always separate us: I remove all the bay leaves from the sauce *before* I serve the spaghetti! Maybe you should try to do the same, Daddy.

So here it is . . . the shocking story that so desperately needed telling has now been told. I remember when I was growing up, you always had the last word. There was no question about it. Your word was final. Well, now the tables have truly turned, haven't they? Thanks to this book, for once in his life, Daddy's Boy gets the real last word! So, ha!

> Fondly,
> your son,
> Chris Elliott

P.S. Some photographer called me the other day and said that they needed you and me together for a photo shoot for the cover of this book. I thought maybe we could wear polo shirts and ascots. Would it be okay with you if I set up the photo shoot for next Wednesday?

Rebuttal to Epilogue

Dear Chris,

Am back in New York after an unrestful summer in Maine. Received your little epistle, and Wednesday is fine for the cover-photo shoot. Let me know what time it will be. Do we have to bring our own ascots or will they be provided?

Your mother wanted me to ask you if you were free for dinner next Friday. (She is making the stuffed pork chops you like so much.)

I spoke with the publisher this morning and they want us to take some seminars on book promotion down at the New School. I think it would be wise, as we are planning to do the talk show circuit and we want this little potboiler to hit the *Times* best-seller list, right?

Hey, I picked up a copy of your Elvis book, and your mother and I enjoyed it thoroughly. We laughed all the way through. It *was* supposed to be funny, wasn't it?

See you Wednesday,
Dad

P.S. It just occurred to me that in the first chapter of *DADDY'S BOY* you claim to have been the tenth son born to the Elliott Clan and that your older brothers were all named Bob, Jr., One through Nine "with the exception," you write, "of the twins, who were fifth in line and named Bob, Jr., Numbers Five A and B." Well, even by

141

simple mathematics, that would mean that there were already *ten* sons when you were born, not nine, and that you were actually the *eleventh* son born to me, not the tenth. Perhaps you should have the editor fix that before the book goes to print. (Unless, of course, you feel that your readers are not intelligent enough to catch the error. I'll leave it up to you.)

P.P.S. One last thing. I hate to bring this up. I know it's like rubbing salt in an open wound, but it seems to me that by the mere placement of my epilogue rebuttal in this book, I have, as usual, gotten the last word! So double ha ha on you!